T0167660

FREEDOM
or TERROR

Europe Faces Jihad

HERBERT AND JANE DWIGHT WORKING GROUP ON ISLAMISM AND THE INTERNATIONAL ORDER

*Many of the writings associated with this
Working Group will be published by the Hoover Institution.
Materials published to date, or in production, are listed below.*

ESSAYS

BOOKS

HERBERT & JANE DWIGHT WORKING GROUP ON ISLAMISM AND THE INTERNATIONAL ORDER

FREEDOM
or TERROR

Europe Faces Jihad

Russell A. Berman

HOOVER INSTITUTION PRESS
Stanford University   Stanford, California

The Hoover Institution on War, Revolution and Peace, founded
at Stanford University in 1919 by Herbert Hoover, who went on
to become the thirty-first president of the United States, is an
interdisciplinary research center for advanced study on domestic
and international affairs. The views expressed in its publications are
entirely those of the authors and do not necessarily reflect the views
of the staff, officers, or Board of Overseers of the Hoover Institution.

www.hoover.org

Hoover Institution Press Publication No. 587

Hoover Institution at Leland Stanford Junior University,
Stanford, California, 94305-6010

First printing 2010
16   15   14   13   12   11   10   9   8   7   6   5   4   3   2   1

Manufactured in the United States of America

The paper used in this publication meets the minimum
Requirements of the American National Standard for
Information Sciences Permanence of Paper for Printed
Library Materials, ANSI/NISO Z39.48-1992. ⊗

Cataloging-in-Publication Data is available from Library of Congress
ISBN 978-0-8179-1114-0 (cloth : alk. paper)
ISBN 978-0-8179-1116-4 (e-book)

*The Hoover Institution gratefully acknowledges
the following individuals and foundations
for their significant support of the*
HERBERT AND JANE DWIGHT WORKING GROUP
ON ISLAMISM AND THE INTERNATIONAL ORDER

Herbert and Jane Dwight
Stephen Bechtel Foundation
Lynde and Harry Bradley Foundation
Mr. and Mrs. Clayton W. Frye Jr.
Lakeside Foundation

Contents

Foreword

For decades, the themes of the Hoover Institution have re-
volved around the broad concerns of political and economic
and individual freedom. The cold war that engaged and challenged our nation during the twentieth century guided a good
deal of Hoover's work, including its archival accumulation
and research studies. The steady output of work on the communist world offers durable testimonies to that time, and
struggle. But there is no repose from history's exertions, and
no sooner had communism left the stage of history than a
huge challenge arose in the broad lands of the Islamic world.
A brief respite, and a meandering road, led from the fall of
the Berlin Wall on 11/9 in 1989 to 9/11. Hoover's newly
launched project, the Herbert and Jane Dwight Working
Group on Islamism and the International Order, is our contribution to a deeper understanding of the struggle in the Islamic
world between order and its nemesis, between Muslims keen
to protect the rule of reason and the gains of modernity, and
those determined to deny the Islamic world its place in the
modern international order of states. The United States is
deeply engaged, and dangerously exposed, in the Islamic
world, and we see our working group as part and parcel of
the ongoing confrontation with the radical Islamists who have
declared war on the states in their midst, on American power

and interests, and on the very order of the international state system.

The Islamists are doubtless a minority in the world of Islam. But they are a determined breed. Their world is the Islamic emirate, led by self-styled "emirs and mujahedeen in the path of God" and legitimized by the pursuit of the caliphate that collapsed with the end of the Ottoman Empire in 1924. These masters of terror and their foot soldiers have made it increasingly difficult to integrate the world of Islam into modernity. In the best of worlds, the entry of Muslims into modern culture and economics would have presented difficulties of no small consequence: the strictures on women, the legacy of humiliation and self-pity, the outdated educational systems, and an explosive demography that is forever at war with social and economic gains. But the borders these warriors of the faith have erected between Islam and "the other" are particularly forbidding. The lands of Islam were the lands of a crossroads civilization, trading routes and mixed populations. The Islamists have waged war, and a brutally effective one it has to be conceded, against that civilizational inheritance. The leap into the modern world economy as attained by China and India in recent years will be virtually impossible in a culture that feeds off belligerent self-pity, and endlessly calls for wars of faith.

The war of ideas with radical Islamism is inescapably central to this Hoover endeavor. The strategic context of this clash, the landscape of that Greater Middle East, is the other pillar. We face three layers of danger in the heartland of the Islamic world: states that have succumbed to the sway of terrorists in which state authority no longer exists (Afghanistan, Somalia, and Yemen), dictatorial regimes that suppress their people at home and pursue deadly weapons of mass destruction and adventurism abroad (Iraq under Saddam Hussein, the Iranian theocracy), and "enabler" regimes, such as the ones in Egypt and Saudi Arabia, which export their own problems with radical Islamism to other parts of the Islamic world and beyond. In this context, the task of reversing Islamist radicalism and of reforming and strengthening the state across the entire Muslim world—the Middle East, Africa, as well as South, Southeast, and Central Asia—is the greatest strategic challenge of the twenty-first century. The essential starting point is detailed knowledge of our enemy.

Thus, the working group will draw on the intellectual resources of Hoover and Stanford and on an array of scholars and practitioners from elsewhere in the United States, from the Middle East, and the broader world of Islam. The scholarship on contemporary Islam can now be read with discernment. A good deal of it, produced in the immediate aftermath of 9/11, was not particularly deep and did not stand the test of time and events. We, however, are in the favorable position of a "second generation" assessment of that Islamic material. Our scholars and experts can report, in a detailed, authoritative way, on Islam within the Arabian Peninsula, on trends within Egyptian Islam, on the struggle of the Kemalist secular tradition in Turkey, and on the new Islamists, particularly the fight for the loyalty of European Islam between those who accept the canon, and the discipline, of modernism and those who don't.

Arabs and Muslims need not be believers in American exceptionalism, but our hope is to engage them in this contest of ideas. We will not necessarily aim at producing primary scholarship, but such scholarship may materialize in that our participants are researchers who know their subjects intimately. We see our critical output as essays accessible to a broader audience, primers about matters that require explication, op-eds, writings that will become part of the public debate, and short, engaging books that can illuminate the choices and the struggles in modern Islam.

We see this endeavor as a faithful reflection of the values that animate a decent, moderate society. We know the travails of modern Islam, and this working group will be unsparing in depicting them. But we also know that the battle for modern Islam is not yet lost, that there are brave men and women fighting to retrieve their faith from the extremists. Some of our participants will themselves be intellectuals and public figures who have stood up to the pressure. The working group will be unapologetic about America's role in the Muslim world. A power that laid to waste religious tyranny in Afghanistan and despotism in Iraq, that came to the rescue of the Muslims in the Balkans when they appeared all but doomed, has given much to those burdened populations. We haven't always understood Islam and Muslims—hence this inquiry. But it is a given of the working group that the pursuit of modernity and human welfare, and of the rule of law and reason, in Islamic lands is the common ground between America and contemporary Islam.

* * *

It was said of Ziad Jarrah, the young Lebanese thought to have been at the controls of United Airlines Flight 93, which crashed into a field near Shanksville, Pennsylvania, on 9/11, that he never missed a party in Beirut and never missed a prayer in Hamburg. Europe has been both the target of jihadist terror and a spawning ground of homegrown jihadists. In this book, Russell Berman, the renowned Stanford scholar of European cultural and intellectual history, provides a searching and wide-ranging assessment of Europe's response to the challenge of radical Islamism. "One of the paradoxes of the era," he writes, "is that while terrorist violence threatens Europe, some Europeans prefer to direct their animus toward other democratic societies, rather than to name their Islamist enemy." But the battle in Europe between the forces of Islamism and "democratic modernity" is not yet settled, Professor Berman writes. The choice is Europe's to make, and, as he reminds us with superb case studies of England, France, Germany, and the smaller nations of Belgium, Holland, and Denmark, there are "many Europes, with different national traditions and with varying relationships to terrorism and radical Islamism." (A particularly poignant chapter on Bosnia depicts the fate of that sad country caught in a no-man's-land between Europe and Islam and between the tolerance of its old Islamic ways and the new temptations of Islamist extremism.)

The great threat of Islamism is in the realm of ideas, and this book, which straddles the fence between contemporary politics and intellectual history, affirms the centrality of values and of national will. In the immediate aftermath of 9/11, and in the acrimonious debate that surrounded the Iraq war, Europe, in the main, dodged the great choice facing it, averting its gaze from the Islamist radicalism putting down roots among the immigrant populations who had come to Europe from the lands of Islam. The welfare state aided and enabled the jihadists and their radical preachers, who took what Europe had to offer as they stepped forth to do battle against its democratic values. But the tide has begun to turn Professor Berman argues, with both sweep and exacting detail, and it has dawned on Western Europeans that the target of jihadist ideology and practice is not the United States alone. There is both moral and political passion in this book and poise as well. Europe has ceded ground to the Islamists, but the choice, elegantly summed up in Berman's title, Freedom or Terror, is in the hands of Europeans themselves. There is no iron law that decrees the triumph of the Islamists and the defeat of democratic modernity. The outcome will be determined by the national will of each and every European society.

True, the Dutch failed to come to the defense of intellectual freedom when Ayaan Hirsi Ali, a noted activist and parliamentarian of Somali background, provoked the wrath of the Islamists, but the Danes stood their ground in a crisis triggered by the publication of cartoons depicting the Prophet Mohammed. The French still revere their secular republicanism and of late have mounted a spirited defense of that inheritance. The Swiss have drawn a line against the construction of minarets in their midst, the voters overriding elite opinion and the appeals to economic interest. England once gave the jihadists and their sympathizers enormous leeway, but, on a cruel day in the summer of 2005, homegrown terrorists reminded that society that freedom isn't a suicide pact. The Islamists have conviction and absolutism on their side, but the arsenal of democracy, when deployed, is formidable in its own right. Side by side, in this luminous book, there is concern for Europe's fate and confidence in its ability to defend its modern inheritance.

Fouad Ajami
Senior Fellow, Hoover Institution
Cochairman, Herbert and Jane Dwight
Working Group on Islamism and
the International Order

Introduction

During the near decade since 9/11, Europe has oscillated through a range of stances in relation to the threat of Islamist terrorism. Some Europeans have fought bravely in Afghanistan, and too many good soldiers have given their lives in that most dangerous front in the war on terror. American soldiers carry the heaviest part of the load but, in addition to the important Canadian role, some European allies have made significant contributions. Europeans have also shown leadership on other fronts, especially in their domestic counterterrorism efforts, which have been able to thwart attacks that might have had catastrophic consequences. Intensive intelligence gathering combined with legislation supporting vigorous enforcement have produced success.

However, not all Europeans have stepped forward to defend democratic modernity against the jihadist challenge. Many in fact have been reluctant even to recognize the special character of the threat, let alone to resist it. Key European political leaders of some of our most traditional allies, like Jacques Chirac in France and Gerhard Schröder in Germany, mobilized international opposition to the efforts of the Bush administration to combat terror. Until recently, European governments undercut diplomatic attempts to restrain the Iranian government in order to protect their robust economic relations with the Mullah's regime, and it has been in European political culture where a toxic ideological mixture of anti-Americanism and anti-Semitism has been brewing for some time. One of the paradoxes of the era is that while terrorist violence threatens Europe, some Europeans prefer to direct their animus toward other democratic societies, rather than to name their Islamist enemy.

This book analyzes the European ambivalence toward jihadist terror and the spread of aggressive Islamism. It is especially concerned with European responses to Islamist terrorism. It describes how some Europeans opt for appeasement and apology for terror, while others stand up for freedom. Both sides of the story are crucial, as is the gray zone in between. This book, despite its brevity, presents a sketch of a complex continent of different nations and traditions in order to understand the range of reactions to Islamism. Of course, it can only touch on some exemplary cases to highlight key developments and important events; it would require a much lengthier treatment to cover all of Europe in exhaustive detail. There are many Europes, with different national traditions, and with varying relationships to terrorism and to radical Islamism. Perhaps, in some distant future when the war on terror has been won, historians will be able to provide a comprehensive account of the European responses. Now, in the midst of battle, this book can only offer a sampling.

The varying responses to Islamist terrorism depend on larger, competing narratives about modern European history. One story about Europe involves the defeat of dictatorships, the rise of democracy, and the emergence of free societies. To some extent, this is the American perspective: the First World War ended the Central European monarchies, the Second World War defeated the Nazis and the Fascists, and 1989 marked the victory of liberal democracies over the Soviet empire. The defeat of Communism is also the lynchpin of the narratives commonly held in the countries formerly under Russian control, the world of the "new Europe," to use Donald Rumsfeld's apt terminology. Within this framework, the story of emancipation, the war against jihadist terrorism takes the shape of a continuation of the fight for freedom. No doubt, the weapons have changed, as well as the modes of warfare and certainly the ideologies, but in the end the conflict involves the struggle between forces of oppression and the opportunities for free men and women to live their own lives as they see fit.

Yet there is an alternative story about modern Europe, which, surveying the past, sees only a series of pointless wars, enormous destruction, and loss of life, and it attributes this infinity of pain and suffering to the excesses of nationalism. This is how Western Europeans often see their past. Nations make war on nations; national traditions are belligerent and provincial. Peace will only come about if we can surpass selfish national loyalties. If only there had been more negotiation and dialogue, if only there had been less nationalism and more cooperation, the pointless killings might not have taken place, and Europe would have been spared the scourge of so many wars. In this account, no ideal is worth a fight, and it is always better to appease in order to avoid conflict. This is a story that does not celebrate freedom and democracy but instead looks forward to a postnational world where international governance resolves conflict through good will and consensus-building.

During the first administration of George W. Bush, these two stories collided head-on and a transatlantic divide on foreign policy emerged, especially with regard to the war in Iraq. Of course that phrasing is an overstatement: the worst of the disagreement took place between the U.S. government and some Western European allies—"old Europe," not "new Europe," and not ever all of the oldsters—but it was nonetheless deep and severe. Bush foreign policy may have imagined extending the wave of freedom that had swept through Eastern Europe and the periphery of Russia into the Middle East: a beautiful vision, no doubt. European leaders, however, were much less eager to see even the most despicable regimes topple, especially when their own economies were so complexly intertwined with Iraq and Iran. One consequence of that divide was the burgeoning of anti-Americanism in parts of Europe, a topic on which I have written in another book published by Hoover Press.*

During the second Bush term and certainly during the Obama administration, transatlantic relations have become less frosty, and on some points concerning Islamism and related topics, Europeans have even begun to speak more assertively than Washington. Perhaps this is just a matter of subtle shifts, but we may also be witnessing a paradigm change and the emergence of a different transatlantic divide. In the years immediately after 9/11, the United States adopted an aggressive posture, while some "old Europeans" seemed unreliable, congenitally predisposed to appeasement. Today that imbalance may have disappeared or even reversed itself: while the U.S. government is doing its best to appear non-threatening, to

---

*Russell A. Berman, *Anti-Americanism in Europe: A Cultural Problem* (Stanford: Hoover Institution Press, 2008).

avoid discussions of terrorism, and to minimize the problem of Islamist violence, the Europeans are growing increasingly concerned about the dangers that surround them.

Some of this shift reflects changing political personalities—Merkel rather than Schröder, Sarkozy instead of Chirac—and some of it results from the Europeans' objective assessment of their greater vulnerability to Iranian missile development. For our purposes here, however, the core issue is the much wider and growing public recognition in Europe of the Islamist threat. This is hardly any wonder: after the 2004 train bombing in Madrid, the 2005 explosions in London, the riots that spread across France in 2005, and the failed bombings and thwarted conspiracies in Germany, the European public has woken up to the dangers in its midst. Add to this the trauma of the murder of Theo van Gogh in the streets of Amsterdam and the shock of the anti-Danish riots throughout the Muslim world in the wake of the publication of the Mohammed illustrations. An irony of history: today, just at the moment when liberal parts of the American political elite would like to pretend that the "war on terror" is obsolete or that jihadist terror is not a war but only a random series of criminal acts, just as some Americans might prefer to be sounding retreat, a critical mass of Europeans is suddenly prepared to begin to get serious about the threat. If 9/11 shocked Americans about the potential of attacks from abroad, the European anxiety has become a fear of homegrown terror, the violence that might emerge from the disaffected immigrant population that has grown in largely isolated quarters or segregated satellite cities, within social systems that do not encourage integration very well. For many Europeans the encounter with Islamist terrorism operates on at least three levels—the wars in Afghanistan and Iraq, the counterterrorism

measures and the scope of police powers Europeans are prepared to tolerate, and finally a range of issues pertaining to
the integration or exclusion of the largely immigrant Muslim
populations. Each country addresses these issues differently
in light of its particular institutions and national history. While
the different Western European countries share basically similar problems, the solutions are always refracted through the
particularities of national histories.

Before turning to the individual national situations, however, this book opens with a consideration of the overall landscape of Europe facing jihad. The focus is on the war of ideas
and the competition of values. We know that there are Islamist
radicals who want to inflict harm and use violence in the name
of nebulous religious claims and extremist goals. The question
is whether Europe has the will to resist. What is the character
of contemporary European culture? Can it muster the strength
to defend its democratic institutions? Or will it succumb to its
own self-doubts and the anxieties of cultural relativism? This
introduction looks at Europe's problems with its own values.
Of course, the erosion of traditions and values is an old story
in Europe, diagnosed extensively by Nietzsche in the late
nineteenth century. Since then European identity, or the individual national identities, have come under additional and
diverse pressures. National cultures have had to face the
crimes of their past from the colonial era or the world wars,
and this process has left them burdened with self-doubts. The
erosion of established religious faith in the large secularist
swaths of Europe combined with the spread of a consumer
culture has also weakened traditional value structures. The
submersion of individual nations into the bureaucracy of the
European Union and the larger slide into globalization has
further reduced national cultures. The result? A postmodern

culture of relativism, with few shared values and diminished symbols of national community, replaced by an ethos of multiculturalism and a reluctance to make "value judgments." Can a Europe tied up by so many hesitations find the strength of will to face a determined enemy?

Nietzsche called the Europe that had lost its values "decadent," and the description surely holds. The paradox remains, however, that despite this cultural enervation and the erosion of identity, there are somehow forces afoot, even in "old Europe," that do find the strength to resist: the soldiers who fight in Afghanistan, the security forces who carry out counterterrorism strategies, and the intellectuals who defend modernity and uphold freedom of speech against those who would crush it in the name of appeasement.

While Europe suffers from a values deficit, the Islamists benefit from their fanatical commitment. We can only imagine that individual terrorists or suicide bombers harbor their own, very private doubts as they go to their death, leaving loved ones behind. We only have suspicions about how they have been manipulated and exploited, seduced by the heroic thoughtlessness of a simplistic ideology. We do, however, know a lot about that ideology, the call to arms to destroy modernity at all costs and to establish a universal Muslim rule. It is on this point that clarity is absolutely necessary. The world religion Islam has existed in multiple forms and cultures, in different times and places in rich and capacious ways. The Islamist version of Islam, the narrow and dogmatic call to violent jihad with the agenda of a reestablished caliphate, is only an extremist and not particularly intelligent interpretation of Islam. It is at best a crude literalism, or not even that, since there is little evidence that the jihadists even command the literacy to read the texts themselves. Claiming to represent the original truth and the authentic tradition, Islamism is in fact a product of a modernizing compulsion that reduces complexity and manipulates the faith to its own ends. While it invokes ancient texts, it integrates them into structures of ideology and repression borrowed from the totalitarian movements of the twentieth century. It is the new communism in its vision of a repressive social utopia, and it is a new fascism in its militarization of life and its chiliastic desire for death. The designation "Islamo-fascism" names this derivation and this brutality.

Our concern, therefore, with Europe's response to Islamist terrorism necessarily involves this Europe, the Europe of multiculturalism and post-traditionalism, decadent Europe, facing this Islamism, frenzied, fanatic, and ideological. Sophisticated self-doubt faces vitality and violence. It is a war of ideas but even more a war of values and a war of will.

But it is also a confrontation in which specific security and social problems require the enactment of realistic policies. It is here that the particular complexity of the European situation becomes clear. After 9/11, the United States was primarily concerned about a threat from abroad; the European discussion has, in contrast, focused on the threat from within, the potential of "homegrown" terrorists emerging from the largely immigrant Muslim communities. This is where precision becomes important. Not only is it crucial to distinguish between Islam and Islamism, it is equally if not more important to avoid confusing the broad Muslim population with the ultimately small cadre of extremist Islamists and their supporters. Such a confusion would be wrong, it would do injustice to most Muslims, and it would play into the hands of the jihadists by pushing moderates into their welcoming arms. (It would also play into the hands of anti-immigrant activists by impugning the loyalty of all immigrants, and thereby distract from the genuine security agenda, identifying the Islamist networks in order to prevent terrorist violence.) Just as the reference to the totalitarianism of the twentieth century helps clarify the character of jihadist ideology, so too can it clarify the relationship between the two populations. In the United States (and elsewhere), the economic and industrial upheavals of the early twentieth century and the social strains of the Great Depression produced widespread activism in the industrial working class, particularly in the form of the union movement. An extremist element, the Communists, who masked their international agenda and their allegiance to a foreign power in a rhetoric of social change, tried to manipulate the much larger working class movement. Its agents sometimes even succeeded in working their way into positions of influence in the unions and elsewhere. There were, however, plenty of unionists who resented the subterfuge, and that era came to an end when they eventually succeeded at expelling the Communists.

That historical lesson is a useful point of reference to understand the dynamic in Europe. The Muslim immigrant communities face a range of social and economic challenges, and the European welfare states have failed to provide effective paths to integration. Disaffection results, and this is where radical jihadist ideology can gain a foothold. Not surprisingly, it is particularly appealing to young men, and this attraction is exacerbated by the gender dynamic of modernization: while young men face Europe's traditionally high unemployment rates, young immigrant women experience European society in terms of new opportunities and the equal rights their mothers did not enjoy. This asymmetrical experience of Europe only makes angry young men angrier and more susceptible to manipulative recruitment networks. Recent news reports confirm a growing number of such recruits—both children of Muslim immigrants as well as converts to Islam from the European population—who are making their way to jihadist training camps in Pakistan. This is the fatal connection between issues of immigration policy and terrorism.

Against this background—the cultural competition between Europe and jihad, and the social policy issues of immigration and terror—the book takes a look at some select cases. Attention is paid to three large countries, historical allies, the real core of "old Europe": England, France, and Germany. Each has experienced terrorism differently. England suffered from the London bombings of 2005, and it was the first country to grapple intensely with the reality of home-grown radicalism. It is also the European country most involved with the paradigm of multiculturalism and the particular issues involved with accommodating multiple traditions. It is not surprising that it was in England that the question of integrating sharia law first emerged. France presents a different model with its legacy of strong republican values, the importance of national identity, and the tolerance for a highly centralized state. On the one hand, the French experience with counterterrorism is exemplary; there is much to be learned from the French success in terrorism prevention. On the other, its management of immigration has produced grievous problems that have erupted into extensive unrest and contributed to the perception of a general breakdown in law and order. All this has been complicated moreover by France's traditional transmediterranean foreign policy opening to the Arab world, which makes explicit critiques of Islamism a sensitive matter, with consequences for the intellectual debates of the past decade. Germany, as so often, lives in the shadow of its past, and the encounter with Islamist terrorism regularly awakens the specters of the Nazi era. For some, that past should make Germany least willing to participate in military enterprises, with the resulting caveats on the role its forces can play in Afghanistan. For others, the erosion of the Weimar Republic by paramilitary extremists makes it all the more incumbent on today's Germany to put an end to terrorism. It is noteworthy that politicians leading the Interior Ministry, from both the center-left and the center-right, have been among the toughest advocates for domestic security measures. Nonetheless, still other Germans draw the lesson from the Nazi era that they should refrain from any criticisms of other religions and other cultures, even if practices in immigrant cultures fail to live up to modern German law. It is telling though that in Germany, as elsewhere, some of the most articulate and dogged critics of abuses in the immigrant communities are themselves Muslim immigrants—progressive, democratic, and dedicated to the ideals of free societies, they articulate the demand that Europeans live up to their own laws and apply those laws equally, to immigrants as well as to everyone else.

After the three discussions of England, France, and Germany, the next chapter travels through three small countries on Europe's north coast: Belgium, Holland, and Denmark. In each, complex histories frame different responses to Islamism. Belgium, with its late but brutal colonial history, has become home to a largely francophone immigrant Muslim population. Belgium also has the dubious honor of having produced the first female European convert to Islam to have carried out a suicide bombing. The chapter focuses on the diversity of responses to Islamism within the immigrant community, as reported by a Flemish-Moroccan journalist who "went underground" to produce a piece of insightful investigative journalism. The case of Holland shows how one of the previously most liberal and tolerant cultures of Europe buckles under the pressure of Islamism. At the center of the story are two friends and collaborators: Theo van Gogh, the cultural critic and gad-fly filmmaker, assassinated in the streets of Amsterdam by an Islamist radical with ties to international terrorist networks; and Ayaan Hirsi Ali, the Somalian refugee who, with deter-mination and intelligence, made her way into an elected seat in the Dutch parliament, promoting the rights of immigrant women and criticizing the patriarchal character of Islam. For her speech, she has faced death threats and was forced into hiding. The chapter also discusses an Iranian exile, Afshin Ellian, like Hirsi Ali, a progressive critic of Islamist reaction, who calls on the West to enforce the most rigorous standards of secularism in politics. This itinerary concludes in Den-mark—on a per capita basis, Danish forces have suffered, af-ter Canada, the most losses in the Afghanistan war—with a discussion of the 2005 publication of the cartoons of Moham-med and the consequences. While the initial reaction to the cartoons was nil, a group of Danish imams took the publica-tion and, enhancing it with other unrelated material, traveled to the Middle East to draw attention to them. Violent riots ensued. Yet it was not only Muslims who objected to the cartoons. Many multicultural Europeans also tried to distance themselves. The Danes nonetheless stood firm, and the gov-ernment insisted on the principle of free speech. In this case, the integrity of a Western institution was upheld, despite the not inconsiderable voices calling for appeasement.

A final case study looks at a very different country: Bos-nia. Here the Muslim community is indigenous, with a history stretching back to the days of Ottoman rule. In that sense alone, Bosnia is quite different from the other European cases, in which Islam is nearly exclusively an immigrant phenomenon. Yet Bosnia is different in another crucial way: the shadow of the wars that followed on the breakup of Yugoslavia and especially the genocidal campaigns against the Bosniaks that culminated in the 1995 killings at Srebrenica. That experience still casts a shadow on Bosnian culture and politics, but it also embodies aspects of the international issues at stake. To talk about Islamist terrorism in Europe—the Madrid bombing, the London bombings, the efforts to bomb in Germany—also requires attention to the genocide in Bosnia. That genocide represented in many ways a failure of Europe, of Western Europe, to live up to its own post–World War II credo: no more genocide. The modernity that jihadists have been attacking since 9/11 (and before) is the same modernity that failed at Srebrenica, and it is no mistake that jihadists list the persecution of Bosnian Muslims in their litany of examples of Muslim suffering—Chechnya, Kashmir, Gaza, Iraq—to justify their own violence. That the Bosniaks themselves, to date, have not succumbed to the jihadist seduction is a testimony to the integrity of their tradition. Nonetheless the battlefields of the Balkans have been more than literary references in jihadist propaganda: they have also served as way stations in the bloody pilgrimages of international Islamist fighters, from the anti-Soviet resistance in Afghanistan, through Bosnia, and into Western Europe. This chapter looks at the complexity of the Bosnian responses to the war and genocide, and the redefinition of Muslim identity in postwar Sarajevo through examples from contemporary Bosnian culture. Bosnia is not London, Paris, or Berlin, but its mixture of violence and religion, modernization and tradition, provides a useful mirror. It too is part of the full story of European responses to Islamist terrorism.

The view of European history as a trajectory to democratization is not wrong: the Kaisers are gone, the Führer is gone, and so are the Soviets. The military and political accomplishments of the twentieth century built on a cultural tradition, which, in different ways in different countries, gradually placed ever greater value on the individual and the freedom of choice. While individuals live in isolation nowhere, and obligations and responsibilities define our lives in communities, there remains a specific Western legacy of individuality, autonomy, and freedom. Today that freedom finds its expression in the ideas and structures generally associated with modernity, no matter how much traditional forms also contribute to our culture: here, too, a range of outcomes is only natural given the diversity of societies and institutions.

It is, however, that modernity and that freedom that are under attack by the agenda of jihadist terrorism. That is no interpretation or insinuation but a clear restatement of their goals. This book asks how Europe is responding to this challenge. Will it defend freedom against terror? And with what urgency? Does it intend to win? The chapters in this book highlight some of the possible answers. Whether Europe is truly up to the challenge will only become clear in the struggles of the next decade.

CHAPTER ONE

European Values and Islamist Violence

Decadence Meets Force

The encounter between contemporary Europe and Islamist terrorists has multiple dimensions. It has involved recent military deployments in Afghanistan and Iraq and, over decades, throughout the Middle East. Yet terrorism is not a war with clear frontlines or uniformed combatants, so another dimension of this encounter involves the extensive counterterrorism strategies carried out within Europe, the painstaking intelligence gathering, and the police actions against jihadist networks. Those steps, however, quickly begin to raise issues of civil liberties that, in different ways and in different countries, touch on the basic values of modern European liberal democracies and become flashpoints of public controversy. We will examine these matters in later chapters, looking at individual European countries and their specific responses. Yet ultimately the question of European responses to Islamist terrorism is a question of culture: the confrontation of contemporary European culture with the cultural values of jihadist radicals. This chapter examines the key fault lines in that confrontation.

The two sides do share some underlying features, in particular the impact of globalization, although this plays itself
out in markedly different ways. For Europe, globalization puts
intense pressure on its values tradition: the cooperation with
the illiberal societies of the non-European world through the
structures of international trade tends to undermine European
values, and the impact of immigration into Europe only
amplifies Europeans' doubts about the integrity of their
traditions. For various reasons—for Germans, it is the memory of the Nazi era, for others it is a sense of guilt from
historical colonialism, in general an epidemic of political correctness—Europeans are often unwilling to stand behind their
values, especially the values of liberal democracy, and to defend them.

Instead, there is an easy slide into cultural relativism:
women's rights, for example, are largely recognized to have
validity within Europe, but Europeans are very apprehensive
about making claims that such rights should apply elsewhere.
Globalization, one could say, makes Europeans decadent, as
far as values go. In contrast, globalization intersects with jihadism in an antithetical fashion, magnifying its aspiration to
establish a transnational regime based on its imagination of
archaic Islam. At stake, of course, is not the Islam that most
Muslims practice, and it is certainly not the traditionalist Islam
that has gradually made accommodations to modernity: rather,
jihadism, as a modern movement, invents a primitive vision,
which it wants to impose on modernity. The jihadist activists
recruit internationally for their universal movement, and they
have been reaching out particularly to disaffected members of
the Muslim immigrant communities in Europe. This is precisely where the encounter of European decadence and jihadist

vitality is so ominous: Europe, unsure of itself, has little to offer in terms of values, while jihad promises paradise.

This chapter investigates the two sides of the encounter. It begins with an examination of the erosion of European values in the context of globalization, and then it turns to the transnational aspirations of jihadism and its own totalitarian resonances. While jihadism confronts Europe and challenges it, in fact it also borrows from Europe, including elements of the worst aspects of the European twentieth century. To understand how Europe responds to the violence of terrorism, it is important first to trace how its own values traditions have been weakened.

The Values Crisis of Globalization

In recent years, questions of values and cultural conflict have frequently occupied the center of public discussion on both sides of the Atlantic, and these debates have taken on varied political shadings. The German discussion of a *Leitkultur*—the idea of a national culture to which immigrants should assimilate—and, similarly elsewhere in Europe and in the United States, the politicized expectation that immigrant populations acquire some familiarity with the language, culture, and values of the host country have often reflected underlying conservative assumptions. In contrast, in France, the adamant defense of a national identity defined in terms of republican values has historically been more a matter of the left and its tradition of adamant secularism, even if conservative politicians have recently taken up the issue. More generally, advocacy on women's issues and human rights have typically tended to arise on the left (even if, in an interesting political development, they too have begun to slide toward the right).

This political indeterminacy makes the topic of political values all the more interesting. Evidently, the question of values does not lend itself to easy political categorization. A broader account is called for to explain how Western political cultures—with their own internal range of positions and hardly monolithic—face sets of pressures in the context of globalization: immigration is only one dimension of a framework that includes enhanced international trade, new global media (the Internet), and global environment questions, not to mention security and energy policies, even if debates typically erupt most dramatically around immigration-related topics and, of course, in response to terrorism. Do Europeans have a body of values they are prepared to defend against terrorist challenges?

If the shared values of the European tradition have grown weak, this is a result of the restructuring of the international order. The wider global context diminishes the standing of local narratives and undermines their stability. Given that degree of generality, there is no reason to assume that there is one single policy solution that would apply uniformly in different countries and to different topics. In later chapters, we will look at the configuration of immigration, terrorism, and cultural change in different national contexts. What we might achieve here at the outset, however, is a framework for comparative discussions of related if nonetheless distinct topics in varied circumstances. There are core questions about shared values that recur in different countries, even if they are answered differently.

Should societies expect new immigrants to internalize the host culture, and, if so, what is the degree of appropriation that could be set as a norm: thorough? partial? minimal? A *Leitkultur* expectation, for example, that all immigrants reach

university-level knowledge of host culture history is surely
unachievable, but that does not imply that assimilation expectations should be lowered to zero. Culture is, after all, not
only distant history but also the way one lives in historically
formed institutions. Should there be any educational outreach
to explain to immigrants the legal rights they can enjoy? Such
rights may not have applied in their countries of origin and
therefore represent something distinctive about the host environment. Assuming the host culture takes its own rights seriously (perhaps an inappropriate assumption), it ought to be
willing to explain them. Sharing good news cannot be bad:
but then what about the host-country history that led to those
rights? The traditions and struggles, heroes and heroines, that
spread rights we may take for granted? That too should be
part of the cultural outreach to new members of the community. For if immigrants do not have access to knowledge of
their rights—which are surely not fully separate from cultural
values and their historical evolution—then discrimination
against immigrants and, in response to that, an attendant radicalization of immigrants can only follow. In other words,
to refrain from pursuing any project of cultural integration
necessarily leaves immigrants vulnerable to exploitation and
practically stripped of their rights. That is the point where
superficial multiculturalism, fearful of denigrating other cultures and therefore unwilling to assert the host culture's
advantages, in effect traps immigrants in marginalized ghettoes, easy prey for the purveyors of radicalism.

Yet if one concedes that immigrants might benefit from
knowing that the host society values nondiscriminatory labor
practices, and that, therefore, if they face discrimination they
would have some recourse in the courts and, even more importantly, that they should have a working knowledge of how

to obtain it, should not the same immigrants also know that the host society similarly values women's rights? What about free speech or gay marriage or religious tolerance? It surely cannot be the case that the rule of law could accept providing an immigrant woman with protection against mistreatment in host-culture institutions while withholding that protection in the context of the immigrant community. Nor does it make sense to provide gays (whether immigrant or not) with the promise of protection against violent attacks by members of the host culture but ignore violence in the immigrant community. Those consequences would, however, result directly from inappropriate bashfulness about the host culture and its Western values. If European nations fail to stand up for their core values at home, it is difficult to imagine how they could participate robustly in the war on Islamist terrorism abroad— and if they jettison their values and dodge the challenge of terrorism, they are not likely to defend their freedom anywhere.

The Western Values Crisis

Ultimately, therefore, the crucial question for us is not immigration and what immigrants should know about their host countries—as important as that may be—but rather why Western societies turn out to be strangely embarrassed about their own value contents. All these desiderata—antidiscrimination, free speech, the equality of women—are enlightenment legacies, established through social conflict and cultural change, and they are consequently embedded in complex and deep histories of controversy, some distant and some—think of gay marriage—very contemporary. None of these achievements of emancipation was easily won, and, when all is said and done, none has ever been fully accepted; there has always been a noticeably repressive undertow eager to limit freedom. Gay marriage is just the most current example, but the backlash against feminism is hardly a secret, and anti-Semitism never disappeared from the secular and tolerant modernity of Western Europe. Similarly, before we celebrate Western advocacy for something as seemingly irreproachable as free speech, let us remember how quickly Western institutions were prepared to cave in on the defense of the publication of Salman Rushdie's controversial 1988 novel, *The Satanic Verses*, when it was condemned by the Ayatollah Khomeini.

While support for the structures of emancipation has never been wholehearted, that does not mean that freedom was just a sham (that theory would be tantamount to the old Communist claim about "bourgeois freedoms" being merely abstract). It does, however, recognize that the reign of freedom is tenuous. If it is not embraced and defended vigorously, it can wither. Especially today, in the context of globalization, freedom faces opponents, and it needs stalwart advocates. Freedom's friends should mount that defense without apologies and despite the enhanced interaction with societies that do not similarly value freedom. Will Western societies, with their specific enlightenment legacies, but now facing a global context that includes significantly repressive cultures and political systems, choose to adjust to the new world order by ratcheting down their own values? It might seem opportune to give up on freedom in order to get along with powerful trading partners in this unfree world. Does an anti-emancipatory global context mean that Western cultures should roll back their own rights? Should Europe become more like Russia and China in order to do business with them more efficiently? Should the West emulate Saudi Arabia in order to ensure an uninterrupted flow of oil?

The suggestions sound absurd, but we should not be oblivious to the waning persuasiveness of Ronald Reagan's invocation of the Puritan imagery of the "City on the Hill" as an example for the world. In the wake of the Iraq war (which, despite its success, was notoriously unpopular) and after decades of cultural relativism, the bold agenda to see the world reborn in our Western image is less radiant than in the glory days of the end of the Cold War. It may even be that a reverse effect has set in: a preemptive apprehension against any judgment that might imply that other societies should become free. Yet if we give up on the expectation that other societies may strive toward freedom, we will surely lose our own. As the West grows more willing to accommodate dictators, we increasingly run the risk of being remade in the image of the non-Western world by adopting its illiberal structures.

To understand the relationship of cultural norms to the challenge of terrorism, we must pay attention to the very value of values. The term implies, correctly, that humans live in cultures where values are in play: our values are not frozen or simplistic, nor are they, however, fully atomized and privatized. Values operate somewhere between the extremes of absolutely singular and infinitely malleable. These cultural goods, the standing of which is at least partially subjective—hence our stereotypical anxiety about "value judgments" because of a misplaced reluctance to insist on something as allegedly subjective as values—face a more objective, notionally quantifiable version of value, understood as worth or even cost. "What is the value of values?" means "What is the cost of having a culture?" or "Are the goods, allegiances, and principles that one holds dearly—one's values—important enough, valuable enough, to imply a willingness to defend them?" While the verb "defend" may provoke angst due to a possibly belligerent connotation, the word does not necessarily imply military defense, although at times that too might be valuable or even necessary. For now, however, let us only consider an argumentative defense or a political defense. We must ultimately ask whether there is any substantive content, any imaginable value, which we should defend or—and this is the stark alternative—are "values" simply not worth the effort? Not worth the effort because we imagine that we could achieve some greater profit if we could overcome the limitations imposed by seemingly arbitrary value allegiances

One can address values in terms of individual character, and important topics of moral evaluation and ethical life would be on the table. We may admire someone who has the character to stand on principle, or—this is always the nagging worry in such cases—perhaps that hardheaded moralizer is just being stubborn and inflexible. Or we can certainly be suspicious of another type, someone who always only seeks out strategic advantage, unless we were alternatively to admire that acquaintance's flexibility, the agility of an opportunist never constrained by commitments. In common parlance, one often appreciates knowing where someone else "stands," because we value clarity, and there is a commonsensical rejection of individuals who are "two-faced"—those who hide their values or motivations or who say one thing here and something else over there. Yet a century of psychoanalysis has taught us nothing if not that there are always ulterior motives, especially multiple and often mutually incompatible desires, unknown even to the actor, which, however, suggests that every principle or value is also a repression, a refusal of competing thoughts and desires. However, not even psychoanalysis would regard that insight into the complexity of the psyche as an argument against values, or against the value of values. We have values in order to act as ethical individuals, but social processes may erode our commitment to those values.

Individual ethics is one matter, but there is also a geopolitical version of this problem of flexibility and adjustment. Western energy policy—driven by so-called postmaterial values—has limited the development of fossil fuels and significantly blocked the development of nuclear energy options. This strategy, however, has only enhanced Western dependence on regimes in areas of the world rich in oil and gas, and poor in enlightenment values. The greening of Western Europe has meant a growing dependence on energy sources elsewhere: Russia and the Arab world. The pressure to accommodate their illiberalism through a reduction in democratic expectations will only grow. Do you bite the hand that feeds you fuel? Proposals by figures as influential as New York Senator Charles Schumer to acknowledge the legitimacy of Russian ambitions in Eastern Europe is a taste of things to come, cut from the same cloth as Russian energy politics in what used to be the New Europe.

Values: Local and Global

We have values as individuals and as members of communities. Here, however, the primary concern is neither the morality of individual value choices nor the values side of geopolitics, but rather the standing of values in contemporary Western, especially European, societies in light of the context of globalization and the Islamist challenge. This is one specific part of the values landscape and, to discuss it, let us focus on the social dimension in between the individual and the geo-political, the particular and the general, in terms of the public debates and institutional articulation of values. How are values discussed in public? What public judgments are made? And more importantly: how can we characterize the transformation of the character of public value judgments as they are impacted by globalization?

The answer to this question requires distinguishing between two models for the operation of values, one is opportunistic and strategic, the other is mimetic and transformative. In both cases, contemporary Western society is understood as composed of multiple actors with various, even conflicting, values, which are in constant evolution. There is no assertion of some unchanging essence of identity—values do change. They change, however, in ways we can describe and that indicate different responses to globalization.

In the first type of values interaction with globalization, the occasion of a specifically "global" reaction (that is, a largely distant and typically hostile reaction) to particular events provides an opportunity for local actors to pursue a strategic agenda. For example, news of a distant response to this or that policy (or some other expression taken as symptomatic of a society, such as a work of art or business venture) is appropriated in the service of a domestic political program. The simple version of this pattern is regularly apparent when accounts of criticism of this or that U.S. policy, or even just foreign public opinion polls regarding attitudes toward the United States, are turned into vehicles for domestic political competition. To be sure, this is a particular U.S. issue, reflecting the highly partisan domestic political environment and the near obsolescence of bipartisanship in foreign policy: the global becomes the local in the next news cycle. World affairs are spun so as to serve best as pretexts for local competition. This is typically the case, for example, when the Pew Research Center issues a report that reveals, one more time, how the United States gets low grades in some countries (the high grades elsewhere are typically underplayed). This provides an opportunity for critics to gain some leverage in their arguments against the administration or a government agency: because X percentage of the respondents in country Y see the United States negatively, it is deemed urgent to modify policy Z. The flaw in the argument is that there may be other rationales, let alone domestic traditions, that make policy Z not only plausible but also even valuable within a realist assessment of national interest. Policy formation—determining the value of Z—can hardly be limited to appeasing those global sensibilities that have allegedly been determined by some polling question.

Of greater interest than reactions to opinion poll data are the dynamics at work around some of the more dramatic controversies of the past decades. The tepid response in parts of the political leadership to the fatwa against Salman Rushdie gave expression to an underlying disregard, to say the least, for literature and the importance of defending the freedom of expression, but matters were in fact worse with important and influential institutions in Western religious communities that saw the fatwa as an occasion to pursue their own agenda to limit blasphemy and other public denigrations of religion. (In other words: parts of Western society uncomfortable with aspects of freedom seized on the opportunity presented by non-Western critics to try to make the case for limiting freedom.)

This is not the place for a full history of the Rushdie affair, by no means Europe's finest hour, but it would be a rewarding project to trace the failure of that strategy. Why was the caricaturing of Mohammed deemed so reprehensible by some non-Muslims in the West? Western religious institutions are typically fair game for criticism, no matter how extreme. In much of Western Europe, hostile caricatures of Christianity and Judaism face no prohibitions. Yet criticisms of Islam can lead to prosecution. One is free speech, the other is hate speech, although the distinction is difficult to maintain rationally. Needless to add, Christianity and, much more so, Judaism are targets of extensive hostility in parts of the Muslim world. So the opportunistic ecclesiastical refusal to stand with Rushdie when he faced death threats was a failed and self-destructive strategy: it gained Western religious institutions nothing, while they forfeited credibility and reputation.

A more recent example involves the controversy around Pope Benedict's XVI's 2006 Regensburg address in which a quotation from a late medieval commentary on Islam provoked violent reaction in many Muslim countries. It subsequently became clear that the manner in which news of the speech was reported on BBC and other radio programs in South Asia effectively obscured the difference between the Pope's own words and the quotation in his text, and this confusion magnified the hostile reception. Yet this response—the outrage not at Benedict's words but the words that he quoted, as they were broadcast—provided opponents of the Pope and, more broadly, opponents of the Church with a strategic political opening. It is arguable that the character of the news broadcasts was crafted to be incendiary; news media do, after all, benefit from the sort of sensationalist reporting that appeals to certain audiences. In the end, the Regensburg affair involved an intra-Western or "local" values conflict—the Pope has plenty of enemies, and the Church has even more—and this conflict was played out through a global controversy but for strategic domestic reasons. The violent response to the speech could be turned into news that translated into political capital for the enemies of the Church and, presumably, of Benedict himself.

In a third case, the Danish cartoon controversy, discussed in Chapter Five, this international cultural dynamic is incontrovertible. The distant response did not erupt until an identifiable lobbying group, a group of Muslim clerics from Denmark, drummed up hostility abroad. They did so by embellishing the original set of illustrations published in *Jyllands-Posten* with images that had nothing to do with the original event and, indeed, nothing to do with representations of Mohammed at all. The genuine *casus belli* had instead to do with the restrictive immigration policy of the Rasmussen government rather than any values conflict around the cartoons. However, the cartoons, transported into a global context, provided the clerics with an opportunity to pursue their own political agenda. The artificially generated controversy provided a vehicle to strengthen the clerics' position as a group and individually, within Denmark and internationally. Viewed from that point of view, the whole matter has less to do with a genuine values conflict than with a discussion of career strategies in an international context. Acting as self-appointed representatives of a minority group, the clerics seized an opportunity to bolster their own institutional and political position as gatekeepers to an international seal of approval for Danish interests in the Muslim world. In other words, the controversy may have been driven less by great ideas of tolerance and representation than by the ambitions of a small group of imams trying to enhance their power position at a specific juncture in the global economy.

In all these cases, what appears to be a values conflict

between the West and the world turns out to involve something much less essentialistic: particular Western interest groups exploit and manipulate distant opinion in order to pursue a specific domestic political agenda. Indeed, one can surmise that in some instances, the Westerners intentionally manufacture distant opinion for Western consumption. It is not what happens in the streets of Islamabad that matters, but the images of Islamabad on the television sets of Western Europe. In the background, a larger question, which cannot be pursued here, involves how domestic political forces may generally engage with actors overseas in order to influence events so as to maximize their own political opportunities at home. The global context invites political actors to act opportunistically to gain advantages within domestic political competition. The confrontation with Islamism offers plenty of opportunities for these strategies.

Giving Up on Western Culture

The second type of response to the global context goes beyond such strategic opportunism. It is instead mimetic and transformative in the sense that it involves potentially deep-seated transformations of cultural values and practices in order to imitate or at least accommodate global (foreign and international) sensibilities, most saliently, but by no means exclusively, in the form of immigrant subcultures. So while the first model of values in the global framework depended on the invocation of distant responses for instrumental purposes, the second model primarily concerns the local cohabitation of different population groups with different points of cultural orientation. In both cases, the global framework contributes to the erosion of traditional value orientations: in our case, this means the weakening of Western values of individual freedom in order to imitate and appease other cultures.

Immigration is hardly new in Europe. What is at stake today, however, is that unlike earlier eras in which a primary expectation involved the assimilation of culturally different immigrants to the host culture, the ethos of contemporary multiculturalism has reversed this process to call instead for an adjustment of the host culture to immigrant expectations. This reversal, a demotion in the importance of host-culture values, has considerable ramifications. Despite the political rhetoric of integration, Western host societies have significantly reduced their expectation that immigrants should internalize the values of their new homelands. This reduction reflects important cultural shifts, involving both a diminished affection for established or "hegemonic" cultural traditions and a much greater reluctance than in past decades to place significant demands or expectations on individuals, immigrant or not.

Of course, change takes place in both directions—many immigrants do integrate and assimilate, although probably much more so in the United States than in Europe—but there is considerable evidence that the host societies, at least in some sectors, have moved toward adopting immigrant values, displaying a willingness to imitate them and to transform, rather than expecting immigrants to adopt the values of the host society. The result is not some giddy cultural diversity but a potential erosion of existing liberal democratic values, the European tradition, which has become a matter of concern in several areas, most prominently around questions of gender.

In the course of the twentieth century, Western societies moved toward a widely shared expectation of ever greater equality for women. However, the influx of populations from distinctly patriarchal cultures, especially the Muslim world, has begun to have its impact in parts of the administration of the welfare state (for example, de facto acceptance of polygamy as a basis for welfare benefits) and most dramatically in some jurisprudence around the so-called "honor killings": murders of wives or daughters by family members due to the womens' acting on their rights to divorce or their adopting Western lifestyles. Cases of apparent murder have been defined downward to charges of manslaughter or the crimes have been otherwise minimized on the basis of a "cultural defense"—the perpetrator's violence is excused by reference to the traditions of the immigrant culture. To be fair, one should note that this cultural defense has also elicited extensive protest and condemnation; yet its very plausibility in some legal circles is symptomatic of a shift in thinking, an accommodation to immigrant culture—or at least, the values of men within that culture—as part of globalization, and this threatens the legal status of women.

Similarly a 2001 debate in Norway regarding the incidence of rape committed by immigrant men prompted anthropologist Unni Wikan to describe Norwegian women as "blind and naïve" toward non-Western immigrants, to the extent that they do not modify their dress and behavior to take into account immigrant perspectives. She commented, "I will not blame the rapes on Norwegian women, but Norwegian women must understand that we live in a multicultural society and adapt themselves to it." The implication is that the erstwhile Scandinavia of sexual freedom belongs to the bygone twentieth century and should make way for a new culture of modesty in order to meet immigrant expectations. Norwegian women should dress, Wikan suggests, according to the expectations of the immigrant men they encounter in public, rather than in terms of their own needs and choices within the framework of prevailing fashion norms.

Interestingly, other research in Norway by Kristin Skørten suggests that cases of honor killing involving romantic love and marital choice receive wide press coverage and sympathy, while the Norwegian public shows less concern when an honor killing involves adultery and divorce. Public sympathy for victims of honor killings varies, therefore, according to the perception of virtue, in rather traditional terms: the girl who wants to marry out of love against her parents' wishes turns out to be more attractive than the divorcee or the adulteress. This suggests that the rollback in attitudes toward women involves at least two dimensions: the regressive attitudes of immigrant men, whose taste Norwegian women are exhorted to respect, but also an underlying ambivalence in the host population, not as thoroughly committed to women's rights as its most progressive representatives might wish.

Related processes are likely at work in reports of heightened rates of anti-gay violence by immigrant youth in European cities formerly known for their tolerance, and there is no doubt that post–World War II condemnation of anti-Semitism in Europe has been diluted by the impact of Muslim immigration. Muslim immigrant anti-Semitism, which often denies the Holocaust, is eroding the postwar European condemnation of the Shoah. The issue here is not so much how to explain anti-Semitic attitudes in the immigrant population—the answer is complex and has as much to do with politics as with religion—but the willingness of European cultures to revise their own historical understanding and the pedagogy associated with teaching the history of World War II in order to accommodate immigrant sensibilities. As with the question of violence against women, the dynamic of the new anti-Semitism includes a mixture of both an element of accommodation to exogenous values (what immigrants think) and some lingering indigenous legacy (what the local population never stopped thinking).

Values and Community, from Nation to *Ummah* and Islamism

Both models of social values in the global context, strategic and mimetic, operate in the complex rhetorical setting of globalized media. What one says in one context can appear immediately (or very soon after) somewhere else altogether. Consider the sad case of Farouk Hosni, the Egyptian minister of culture, who declared in the Egyptian parliament that he would like to burn Israeli books, standard fare in Cairo. However, it was promptly reported in Paris, where book-burning is not as attractive an image but where Hosni was a candidate to head UNESCO. He backtracked, faced reverse attacks, and backtracked again, and then again. In the fifth round of the 2009 UNESCO vote, Hosni lost to Bulgarian diplomat Irina Bokova.

For all the exaggerated talk of a global community, modern life is not above all communitarian. Far from it. At times it is brilliantly dynamic, replete with new opportunities; at times it involves drastic dislocations and loneliness, and these are two sides of the same process that can be brutally isolating. Ethical life mitigates that ruthlessness through goodness. This is where values become valuable, not on the level of prescribed identity from the political or cultural institutions, which are about as far away from genuine values as one can get. Indeed, a distinctive feature of globalized modernity is the enormous distance between the elite administrative management of society, where values are proclaimed abstractly, and the lived lives of humanity, where values really matter.

Yet it is precisely in this gap, between the official values of European administered society and lived life, that globalization in its various forms undermines a firm sense of values and cultural identity. Europeans have grown—in the sense of the philosopher Friedrich Nietzsche—decadent, having lost faith in a coherent set of ideals. Values have been replaced by a cultural relativism that makes Europeans all too willing to refrain from any value judgment. It is this poverty in values, the weakness in cultural identification, that makes Europe such a vulnerable target to the ambitious vitality of the jihadist agenda. Despite the formal effort to unify Europe into a single union, in fact what is transpiring is the erosion of national collectives and communities of shared values. Jihadists recognize this profound cultural weakness, which motivates their recruitment efforts not only among disaffected immigrant youth but among "native" Europeans as well. Europe may not be able to project an image of a desirable life worth living, but the jihadists can do just that, and while Europeans are reorganizing their continent into a postnational bureaucracy, breaking with their own traditions, Islamism can project a positive agenda for a postnational, universal community of faith in the Muslim *ummah* (community of the believers). Key to an understanding of the European response to Islamist terrorism is precisely this confrontation between alternative models of political space: an increasingly postnational Europe and the transnational aspiration of the Islamist revolutionaries.

The "nation" has been the primary unit of political membership in modernity, typically stronger than "region" (as was demonstrated by the conclusion of the American Civil War in 1865) and almost always stronger than "class" (as Europeans learned in 1914, when the various socialist parties all chose to demonstrate their allegiance to their respective nations, rather than to insist on the socialist utopia of internationalism). Membership in the nation has meant citizenship, the basis of civil rights and civic responsibility within the rule of law. However "nation" is also related to the "people," the source of all democratic power. The "people," as concept, indicated the accumulated inhabitants of the territory in the age of the democratic revolutions before the waves of mass immigration.

While the eighteenth-century enlightenment notion of "the people" was not an ethnic definition, the nineteenth-century romanticization of the term and its metamorphosis into the French *nation* or the German *Volk* initiated an ethnic metamorphosis, leading to a fundamental instability in political categories. Citizenship, as civic membership in the political community, stood at odds with nationality, as membership in a cultural or ethnic group. This tension underlies the introductory passages of Hitler's *Mein Kampf*, for example, where contempt for the state coincides with loyalty to the *Volk*. This conflict implies an antipolitical feature inherent in ethnic nationality because it is precisely the opposite of citizenship. Such cultural identity, outside of the realm of politics, might be treated in parallel to other non-civic terms of identification: economic class, for example. However, it is one thing when nonpolitical identity dimensions remain external to politics, for example, a private sector. It is quite another when the ethno-cultural loyalties surpass and displace citizenship. The antipolitical becomes the political. It is a long road between the formation of nations in nineteenth-century Europe and the twenty-first century conflict with Islamist terrorism, but a key piece of the process involves the character of the political community. As Europe dismantles its nations, as it replaces politics with bureaucracy, the Islamist agenda represents an attempt to provide a substitute politics of authenticity. The less credible European politics becomes, the more compelling the jihadist critique, especially to disaffected youth in and around immigrant communities.

From Ethnic Movements to Jihadist Universalism

The concern here involves a profound deformation of political life: when the community around the state is defined less in civic and more in ethno-cultural terms, that is, the denigration of citizenship and its replacement by a politicized folkhood. Historically, this ethnicization of political membership made up a key element in the mass movements of the late nineteenth and early twentieth centuries. This is precisely the issue that Hannah Arendt addresses in *Origins of Totalitarianism* with regard to pan-Germanism and pan-Slavism. While overseas imperialism involved the establishment of mechanisms of administration over other peoples, the pan-nationalism movements mobilized loyalties across national boundaries, subverting the states they defined. Both expansionary processes, Arendt claims, corrode the viability of the state. The ambitious imperialist expansionism which starts as an expression of modern greed becomes the precursor of Communist and Nazi fantasies of world conquest—and world conquest is, by definition, a category that explodes nationhood. It indicates an explicit disregard for the limitations of national interests and therefore, Arendt would say, it denigrates the citizen as the carrier of rights. The expansionist destruction of the nation means the abolition of the civic individual, and that "end of man" is the genuine totalitarian goal.

Arendt's description of Nazism and Communism, the two

totalitarianisms of the twentieth century, emphasizes their postnational character. One sought world domination in the name of race, the other pursued an equally global agenda in the name of class. This history is of interest in this context because the neo-totalitarian underpinnings of jihadist radicalism display a similar global aspiration: world domination in the name of a God. To date, there is no consensus on the precise designation. "Islamism" suggests a precision that is somewhat forced in its distinction from "Islam," although it is a useful way to distinguish between the political ideology and the religion it tries to appropriate. Alternatively, the term "Islamo-fascism" has been deployed to underscore the connection to a historical radicalism and to focus on the denigration of civil rights and individual freedom.

Some critics oppose the term with the claim that the adjective "Islamic" can have nothing to do with "fascism," let alone terrorism. Yet the terrorists themselves define themselves, rightly or wrongly, in terms of Islamic identity and invoke Islamic teaching. More significantly, the objection that a denominational adjective should not be attached to any political tendency is simply misplaced, since it occurs regularly: Christian Socialism, Jewish Nationalism, Hindu Conservatism—these terms do not suggest that all Christians are socialists, all Jews nationalists, or all Hindus conservatives, but that within those religious-cultural traditions, these political tendencies exist along with others. Hence: Islamic fascists, as opposed to Islamic liberals, Islamic conservatives, and Islamic democrats (and this last group plays a particularly heroic role in the story recounted in this book). Yet if the thesis of terrorism as an Islamo-fascism holds, that means that the European response to Islamist terrorism also involves the continent's renewed confrontation with one of the nightmares of its own twentieth-century past. The fight against Islamist terrorism is today's antifascism.

An opposite objection to the term involves the claim that "Islamo-fascist" is redundant, in the sense that the various repressive, antimodern, and violent tendencies implied by "fascism" are themselves central to Islam in general. In this account, Islam is not at all the "religion of peace," as George W. Bush insistently defended it, but its very opposite. Ironically, this criticism, evidently hostile to Islam, is identical with the radical Islamic interpretation: both view Islam as mandating a violent war against nonbelievers. Opponents and adherents engage in the same celebration of reductionist readings of textual meaning to an unchanging core, which is, when all is said and done, historically not tenable. There is little more unstable than the interpretations of texts. *Habent sua fata libelli*, including the Koran. The meaning of books changes over time.

Islamo-Fascism and Islamist Terrorism

In lieu of a full theory of Islamic fascism, noting some tentative points of comparison with the experience of Nazi Germany is useful. The metanational character of pan-Germanism—this is the key point in Arendt's account—contributes to the dismantling of the political entity of the nation-state, the Weimar Republic, and its democratic institutions. It replaces citizenship with ethno-racial identification, and it paves the way for an unlimited expansionist agenda: the aspiration to build an Aryan empire surpasses the limits of the Weimar Republic. In the postwar era, in the process of decolonization, especially in parts of North Africa and the Middle East, elements of the anticolonial movements drew less inspiration from the classic national unification processes of Europe (associated, for example, with the names of Garibaldi and Bismarck) than from the pan-nationalism movements of ethnic empire. This expansionist agenda, driven by ethnicity and race, overshadows the civic morality of nation-building.

This priority of ethnicity over citizenship explains the relative underdevelopment of specifically national political processes and institutions, which are typically manipulated to serve a larger agenda: for example, pan-Arab ambitions repeatedly overpower Palestinian nationalism, or other local national tendencies, with deleterious consequences for the construction of nation-state institutions, the necessary vessels with which democracy might thrive. Potential citizenship in a set of national institutions that might guarantee rights collapses under the pressure of the loyalty demands of pan-Arabic solidarity or, more recently, pan-Islamic aspirations for the *ummah*. It is this pan-Islamic romanticism that inspires the jihadists, and their sacred universalism provides them with a mantle of dignity that the self-doubting national cultures of Europe no longer generate.

The magnetism of jihadist radicalism, the attraction it can exercise on disaffected youth who become potential recruits, represents a latter-day fascism, which can radiate the same fascinating appeal as did the original fascist movements eighty years ago. Revolutionary heroism, biting cultural criticism, and chiliastic terror revive the aura of the totalitarianism of the twentieth century. This, however, is no mere analogy. Significant aspects of Islamist radicalism have roots that are historically traceable to German imperial and National Socialist ambitions. Part of this history includes the biographies of the various Nazi notables who found safe haven after 1945 in Syria and Egypt, and whose ideological vitriol, the mixture of anti-Westernism and anti-Semitism, eventually filtered down to the cadre of today's terrorists.

However, the larger piece of this history, which links today's Islamist terror to the fascism of the last century, involves the standing of the Middle East in German imperial geopolitics, and the central figure in this story is undoubtedly the "Grand Mufti" of Jerusalem, Amin al-Husseini, the leader of Palestinian nationalism during the British mandate. In the 1920s, al-Husseini initially tried to cooperate with the British but eventually—unlike competing Palestinian groups—staked out a rejectionist position that led him into exile. Instead of pursuing Palestinian national goals, he rapidly subordinated them to a pan-Arab agenda, which he also linked to appeals to Germany after Hitler's rise to power in 1933. The Nazi response to al-Husseini was at first positive but rarely more than lukewarm, since at the time Palestine counted less for German foreign policy than did efforts to keep channels open to England and, later, the desire to avoid conflicts with Italy, which had its own Mediterranean ambitions.

Nonetheless, al-Husseini made the enormously destructive political miscalculation of linking the Palestinian agenda— and his own—to the Nazis, and he got little in return. After 1941 he ended up in Berlin, broadcasting pro-Axis propaganda to the Arab world. He actively lobbied against the few negotiations in which the Nazis considered allowing groups of Jews to emigrate in exchange for German prisoners—al-Husseini indicated that it would be better to send the Jews to Poland (that is, to extermination camps). He was also centrally involved in establishing a division of the Waffen-SS made up of Bosnian Muslims, for which he developed a specific ideological justification, a detailed account of the compatibility of Islam and National Socialism. His Nazi collaboration extended well past the point in time when he could have hoped for a Nazi victory; in other words, this was not a matter of tactical opportunism but the expression of sincere ideological commitment.

The German components of this connection therefore help explain the genealogy of Islamic fascism on two levels. First, in order to appeal to what he perceived to be German interests, al-Husseini expanded the local Palestinian question into a regional pan-Arabism and, second, he provided the ideology for an Islamic fascism through the articulation of the compatibility of Islam and Nazism. This second dimension involves the eradication of individual rights. Nineteenth-century national unification movements typologically established normative civil rights (in Germany, Italy, and, as a distant parallel, the United States through the Civil War and Reconstruction). The transition from civic nationalism to the ethnic pan-nationalism movements undermined these rights, a process that led to the totalitarian dictatorships and the concentration camps. Totalitarianism was not simply the withholding of rights from certain individuals or groups but the eradication of the very notion of that sense of individuality which might claim a right to rights. The ideological expression of this agenda included the trivialized collectivism of Rudolf Jung's phrase "*Gemeinnutz geht vor Eigennutz*" (collective interest over individual interest) from his programmatic exposition *Der Nationale Sozialismus* (1919), which al-Husseini adapted as a core Islamic teaching in his address to the imams of the Bosnian Waffen-SS. More than a platitudinous exhortation to selflessness, the rhetorical act represents an effort to retrofit Nazi platitudes as Islamic dogma. Today, seventy years later, Islamist ideology recycles the same gestures of totalitarianism to terrorize democratic societies.

This displacement of the individual by collective obligation is part of the distinctively illiberal character of the pan-
nationalism movements, including pan-Arabism. The primacy
of the collective means homogenization: the individual has no
rights and freedom disappears. This structural ethnic collectivism means the elimination of diversity. In pan-Arabism it
took the form of the programmatic discrimination against non-
Arab minorities, from the prohibition against the use of the
Berber language Tamazight in Algeria to the attacks on the
Kurds under Saddam and the violence of the Janjaweed militia
in Darfur.

The complex slide during the last third of the twentieth
century from pan-Arabism (in which Christian Arabs still
played prominent roles) to pan-Islamic identity and to Islamist
radicalism needs nuanced exploration. However, it is clear that
neither pan-Arabism nor pan-Islamism leaves much room for
a normative expectation of civil rights. Thus, for example, the
Hamas Charter only mentions the term "right" in article 7, but
there it is the movement that has a "right," not an individual.
From the priority of the movement, it follows that women, in
article 18, are only described in terms of family and household
responsibilities, albeit with a particular access to politics:
"good mothers . . . aware of their role in the battle of liberation." The statement is a logical consequence of the prece-
dence of common interest over individual interest. It is an
indication of the stark contrast between the ideologies of Islamist terror and the Western tradition of freedom, let alone
expectations for gender equality.

Freedom or Terror

To analyze the European responses to Islamist terrorism requires us also to think the reverse: how does Islamist terror

judge Europe? The issue is not merely the technicality of how to carry out bombings, nor can the question be reduced to a kind of sociological pathology: what conditions of disadvantage cause the terrorist to make the fateful decisions? Those matters are, of course, not without interest, but the key point must be the destructive idealism, the desire to destroy the world in order to redeem it, that drives the terrorist to engage in the sacred violence of the chiliastic movement. This is ultimately also an inheritance from European totalitarianism: while the jihadists present themselves as direct heirs to an Islamic truth, a Salafist desire to return to the origins of the faith, in fact they also thrive on the legacies of twentieth-century political violence in its ugliest forms.

The redemptive utopias of fascism and Communism, laid to rest in 1945 and 1989, respectively, return from the grave in the guise of Islamism. They are the undead, the specter that haunts Europe today and aspires to bring the realm of freedom to an end. On the surface they seem to have so little to offer. Nonetheless they have a strength, not merely in attracting the disaffected and marginalized, alienated youth who can be manipulated into committing suicide attacks. Much more important is the direct confrontation, in the realm of culture and ideas, with the values of the West and the great traditions of Europe. It is here that the real battle is played out. It is not because the jihadists have a good so precious that they are a powerful adversary; it is not because they have a compelling case or irrefutable ideas. It is rather that Europe, where the advocacy of freedom should be strongest, is gripped by its own crisis of faith and self-doubt. Compared to the alienation of postmodern Europe, the vitality of jihadist radicalism radiates strength, even if its ideas do not stand up to critical scrutiny. The question for the future is whether Europe will stand up to defend its own ideas and identity with comparable vigor.

In the face of a new totalitarian movement, oriented toward world conquest, antithetical to individual life, and enamored with death, modernity is struggling to name and understand the radicalism of its opponent. The examples of the twentieth century, the anti-individual internationalisms of race and class, may not be directly identical—analogies are always only approximate—but our knowledge of the past provides useful first steps toward an understanding of what we face today.

CHAPTER TWO

England

Rights and Traditions

On Wednesday, July 6, 2005, the International Olympic Committee, meeting in Singapore, voted to accept the proposal to hold the 2012 Olympic Games in London. A crowd of 15,000 gathered in Trafalgar Square celebrated the announcement of the first London games since 1948. The city was elated.

The next day, at 8:50 A.M., in the midst of the morning rush hour, a series of suicide bombings by Islamist terrorists left 52 dead, some 700 wounded, and a city in shock. Three of the bombs went off in the Underground, one on a double-decker bus. In the wake of the high-profile attacks in New York and Washington, D.C., on September 11, 2001, in Bali on October 12, 2002, and the train bombing in Madrid on March 11, 2004, a watershed day of terror, "7/7," had arrived in London. The stark contrast between the joyful celebration of the previous day and the stunning pain of the attack made matters even worse. As British novelist Ian McEwan wrote, "The mood of a city has never swung so sharply. On Wednesday there was no better place on earth. After the victory in Singapore, Londoners were celebrating the prospect of an explosion of new energy and creativity. . . . But terror's war on us opened another front on Thursday morning. It announced itself with a howl of sirens from every quarter. . . . The mood on the streets was one of numb acceptance, or strange calm." How did England respond?

Beyond the pointless deaths, the horror of explosions in the subways, and the panic in the streets, what particularly shocked the British public was the identity of the terrorists, all of whom perished in the attacks. While the terrorism of 9/11 in the United States had been carried out by Arabs from the Middle East—15 from Saudi Arabia, two from the UAE, and one each from Egypt and Lebanon—all of the attackers of 7/7 were British: at stake now was the uncanny encounter with the danger of a "homegrown terrorism." The initial responses to the London bombings did not lead to stories about Britain facing an assault from abroad; the American narrative of a homeland endangered by agents from abroad did not pertain—in that sense, 7/7 was not a replay of 9/11. The British could not retreat into a cozy feeling of national solidarity. On the contrary, the threat of Islamist terrorism had now taken a terrifying and disconcerting turn, as it revealed itself to be a danger germinating within British society itself.

This was disturbing and unsettling: immigrant youth who knew British culture from the inside had turned against their own country. Facing this perplexing development, public opinion needed compelling answers that would somehow provide reassurance. A debate ensued: were the attacks linked to international networks of jihadists or were they solely a matter of disaffected youth? And which of those alternative hypotheses would be preferable? Attributing culpability to small groups of foreign agents might tend to exonerate the large immigrant communities, but discovering the long arm of Al Qaeda reaching into the London subway could hardly be a source of comfort. If, however, the bombings derived solely from the alienation of the immigrant community, danger was suddenly much closer to home, no longer banished to distant Afghan caves. Still, the claim that immigrant youth posed the problem could only raise new questions, since one would have to distinguish between vague gestures of protest, designed to grab headlines, and some mature, ideologically driven political agenda. Were the attacks merely the undisciplined workings of a random group of isolated individuals or part of an organized Islamist terrorist network operating in secret within Britain? Just as in the immediate aftermath of 9/11, the American public was driven by a need to determine the identity of the attackers, in Britain too there was an angry and relentless search for explanations.

Parts of the British press took pains to minimize Al Qaeda or other international connections; such a response evidently amounted to a preemptive rejection of an international response by the British government of the sort that the Bush administration had taken by turning promptly to Al Qaeda and the haven that it had found in Taliban-ruled Afghanistan. However, it is by now indisputably documented that at least three of the London bombers had passed through Pakistan— two of them, Mohammed Sidique Khan and Shehzad Tanweer, had been there as late as February 2005, just months before 7/7. Khan is also alleged to have received training from Jemaah Islamiyah, the Indonesian terror group that had carried out the Bali bombing, and he may have helped plan a 2003 bombing in Tel Aviv. So even for homegrown terrorists, an international terrorist background is certain, although it is unclear how much this also applies to the other three bombers: while Khan, presumably the ringleader, was 30 years old, the others were aged 18, 19, and 22. Hasib Mir Hussain, the youngest, had been a member of soccer and cricket teams; Tanweer, 19, had studied sports sciences at Leeds Metropolitan University before leaving for Pakistan. Two of the bombers left pregnant wives behind. While 7/7 can be read in part as an extension of organized international terrorism, it is also a story of a cold-blooded authority figure manipulating much younger men, impressionable and probably unstable.

Khan left a videotaped statement explaining his motivation; it was aired on Al Jazeera on September 1, 2005, less than two months after the attacks. In it he asserted: "I and thousands like me are forsaking everything for what we believe. Our drive and motivation doesn't come from tangible commodities that this world has to offer. Our religion is Islam, obedience to the one true God, and following the footsteps of the final prophet messenger. Your democratically elected governments continuously perpetuate atrocities against my people all over the world. And your support of them makes you directly responsible, just as I am directly responsible for protecting and avenging my Muslim brothers and sisters. Until we feel security you will be our targets, and until you stop the bombing, gassing, imprisonment, and torture of my people we will not stop this fight. We are at war and I am a soldier. Now you too will taste the reality of this situation." Khan's statement combines an assertion of Islamic identity, an insistence on the priority of belief over this-worldly goods ("commodities"), and a political critique, implicitly attacking the democratic West for unnamed policies, no doubt including the British role in the wars in Iraq and Afghanistan. In other words, he justifies the bombing as a response to British policies in the Middle East. (It is worth nothing that 30 percent of the bombing victims on 7/7 were not British—collateral damage in Khan's war on England.)

Interpreting the event involves multiple dimensions: the role of international terrorist networks, the character of a radical Islamist subculture in Britain, degrees of diffuse disaffection in parts of the largely immigrant Muslim population in Britain (1.6 million in a national population numbering 60 million). A poll of British Muslims showed that while 77 percent described the bombings as "not at all justified," 56 percent "understood" why people might resort to the violence of 7/7, and 31 percent agreed that "Western society is decadent and immoral, and Muslims should seek to bring it to an end, but only by nonviolent means." Clearly an overwhelming majority of the British Muslim community condemned the attacks—asked what they would do if they suspected someone of planning a similar attack, 73 percent declared that they would report it to the police—but a significant minority indicated that they felt a distance to the host culture, while a noticeable if small minority conceded an affinity to the bombers: 6 percent described the attacks as "justified." No matter how small that minority, it became a source of anxiety, a sufficient pool of potential recruits for future terrorism: were more attacks incubating within British society?

Two weeks later, on July 21, a second set of bombings was attempted, but the explosives failed to detonate. It was not security forces who had saved the day but the incompetence of the would-be culprits, who were all apprehended. Future bombings had become worrisomely possible. The hypothesis of "homegrown terrorism" gained ground, which turned the debate inwards: something had to be done and someone had to be blamed. Of course, political arguments were made attributing the bombings to British foreign policy and the alliance with the United States, but the primary focus of the British response involved transatlantic politics less than a focus on domestic and cultural matters. In some quarters, a xenophobic suspicion of immigrants and Islam—not only Islamism—developed. Meanwhile the government, with considerable public support, called for stricter security measures. In contrast, those who attributed the violence to the disaffection of minority communities advocated for greater multiculturalism and tolerance, while others clamored for a search for scapegoats.

As dramatically as 7/7 influenced British perceptions of the terrorist threat, it was perhaps more a matter of clarification than profound change. As McEwan asked, "How could we have forgotten that this was always going to happen?" In the background of national consciousness, the memory of the IRA bombing campaign was still alive: terrorist attacks were not new in London. Moreover, the series of Islamist attacks around the world provided no reason to assume that England would be spared, especially given Prime Minister Tony Blair's vocal support for American foreign policy and the role British troops were playing in Iraq. Of course, for all of Blair's popularity, his close relationship with President George W. Bush was nothing if not controversial. Critics of that relationship and of the Iraq war were therefore eager to seize upon 7/7 as an opportunity to attack Blair's foreign policy. The response to the terrorist attacks of 2005 was less a moment of innovative transition than a crystallization of several political and cultural discussions that had been underway for several years, stretching back even prior to 9/11. To understand the British response to Islamist terrorism, it is useful to tease out some different strands that characterize the discussion in the UK, in particular these three: the security response in the form of antiterror legislation and the critique it faced, especially from the human rights community; the concern with immigration, multiculturalism, and the status of British cultural identity, including religion; and, finally, the exacerbation of discourses of anti-Americanism and anti-Semitism, especially on the left and among parts of the British cultural elite. These three intertwined themes—security policy, multiculturalism, and scapegoating—have indelibly marked the political culture of Britain during the first decade of the century.

Counterterrorism and Human Rights

The ambivalence of the British response to terrorism has been nowhere clearer than in the history of antiterror legislation. While the United States, in response to 9/11, focused primarily on an external threat to homeland security or, in contrast, while France has largely emphasized a core national value of secularism, the British discussion has oscillated between anxieties about homegrown terrorists, on the one hand, and international jihadists, on the other. Is the problem domestic or global? Is it a criminal matter or a military threat? At times Britain has responded robustly—it was the one European nation to suspend article 5 of the European Convention on Human Rights, which prohibits detention without trial, an emphatic step to give priority to domestic security, even at the price of pulling back from specific human rights commitments. Yet the British judiciary has been in the forefront of integrating international human rights law into domestic law, undermining the authority of security forces, just as it, more broadly, subordinates national law, rooted in democratic processes, to international agreements. The history of legislation and jurisprudence on terrorism has swung back and forth between amplification of state power and defense of civil and human rights. British institutions and culture remain deeply divided on the proper response.

In response to violence associated with the dispute over Northern Ireland, the Prevention of Terrorism Acts, passed between 1974 and 1989, operated with a narrowly political definition, treating terrorism as "the use of violence for political ends [including] the use of violence for the purpose of putting the public, or any section of the public, in fear." Yet—even before 9/11—the Terrorism Act of 2000 expanded the range of offenses to respond to concerns about violence by activists no longer narrowly political in the sense of attacks against state sovereignty (for example, violence associated with animal rights activists or—drawing from the American experience—antiabortion extremists). It was, however, the Anti-Terrorism, Crime and Security Act (ATCSA), passed in the wake of 9/11—the British corollary to the Patriot Act—that equipped the Home Secretary with the authority to subject foreign terrorists to indefinite detention without a specific charge, if such suspects could not be legally deported. Yet that very limiting condition is indicative of the hybrid combination of enhanced police powers, the power to detain, and concern with human rights: the provision regarding legal limitations on deportation refers to those cases in which the prospect of returning foreign suspects to their home country raises credible concerns that they might be subjected to human rights abuses, including torture or the death penalty. Where such danger exists, deportation was not acceptable, and hence the grounds for unlimited detention.

Eventually, however, the fact that ATCSA subjected only resident foreigners to the possibility of internment without trial—because the whole condition of prohibited deportation has no meaning for British subjects—the law was deemed discriminatory on the basis of the Human Rights Act of 1998. The Prevention of Terrorism Act 2005 remedied this by allowing that "control orders" could be issued against British citizens and resident foreigners alike: that is, the instrument of extended detention could now be used against any suspect, regardless of citizenship. The parliamentary debate, which took place in February and March—before the attacks of 7/7 —was very heated and polarized, particularly because the law was denounced as an erosion of habeas corpus, a protection of the accused deeply rooted in the British legal tradition. At the core was a dramatic dispute over how best to balance the need to provide safety and security to a society facing a terrorist threat and, at the same time, to protect core civil liberties.

The bombings of 7/7 quickly initiated a new round of political debate, however, leading to the adoption of the Terrorism Act 2006. Immediately after the attacks, the Labor government began to pursue new legislation. What distinguished this initiative was a focus on the perceived advocacy for terrorism in radical Muslim circles, in particular at the Finsbury Park Mosque in London, but in other Islamist venues as well. The recruitment of the London bombers, especially the younger ones, was attributed to the polemical speech and publications that circulated in extremist circles. That promotion or encouragement of terrorism was now to be criminalized. In his August news conference, Blair explicitly announced new antiterrorism legislation that would criminalize condoning or glorifying terrorism, and he made a general reference to recent Islamist declarations. He was presumably referring to comments by Omar Bakri Mohammed, a Syrian who had first arrived in Britain in 1986, who had declared 9/11 to be "magnificent," and who had boasted of his Al

Qaeda connections shortly after 7/7. (He left England that summer for Lebanon and is prohibited from returning.) To prevent future terrorism, the government argued, speech that endorses terrorism had to be stopped.

In Parliament however, the central controversy involved the proposed extension of the government's power to detain suspects without charges to a period of ninety days. Proponents argued for the need of this extended police power to prevent future attacks. Opponents feared an extraordinary expansion of police powers, an argument made both by Michael Howard, the leader of the Conservative Party, on the right, and, on the left, by the South African Archbishop Desmond Tutu, who drew analogies to apartheid-era South Africa. In the course of the debate, a poll determined that a considerable majority of the British public (72 percent), deeply concerned with public safety after the underground attacks, supported the 90-day detention. In the end, however, the 90-day term was defeated—a significant blow to Blair—replaced by a 28-day term, which in any case doubled the previously existing 14-day detention. The bill was finalized with Royal Assent in March 2006.

This accelerating history of antiterror legislation and the controversy it engendered gives evidence of a culture deeply torn between a search for security and anxiety about the potential loss of civil rights. What makes the British debate on this matter interestingly different from what transpired in the United States is the political constellation: In England, it was the center-left Labor Party prime minister who advocated for the expanded police power, leaving room for parts of the Conservative Party to object on civil libertarian grounds. Civil libertarian objections to counterterrorism legislation coming from the right gave the British debate a texture very different from the U.S. debates over the Patriot Act. The apt comparison, however, would be to the objections that Republicans raised to efforts to expand federal security powers during the Clinton administration.

National Identity and Multiculturalism

Parliamentary debates and legislation are crucial in guiding society, as are judicial decisions; nor, however, can there be any doubt that society is larger than legislation and political platforms and that to understand the reverberations of terrorism in England, it would be shortsighted to ignore changes in the wider culture. For in the late twentieth century, England, as much as any other Western European country and perhaps even more so, witnessed a destabilization of a primary national identity and its displacement by variously unstable, postmodern, and multicultural paradigms. Of course, the concept of a singular national identity was itself largely a nineteenth-century invention, a product of the era of classical nationalism. For many Western Europeans, the world wars of the twentieth century represented the direct consequence of that nationalist legacy, which in turn implied the urgency of renouncing traditional national identity—whether by turning to structures of international governance or through strategies of multiculturalism. For many enlightened and progressive Europeans, any firm national identity, let alone a positive sense of tradition or patriotism, was a problem to be solved through the adoption of alternative identities and affiliations.

Yet that older sense of nationhood had also been part and parcel of the rise of modern democracy, the political theory that located the origins of sovereignty in the people of the nation. The concept of the "nation" was very much connected to the rise of democracy (a connection that plays a large role in the French allegiance to republican values, as the next chapter will show). Prior to the rise of democratic modernity, populations of territorial states embraced diverse local traditions and maintained social hierarchies. In addition, even in that age of nineteenth-century high nationalism, the identity of the British population was complex—not only due to the diversity of legacies in the British isles—Welsh, Irish, Scots—but also because this was simultaneously the age of empire. Intra-European immigration brought waves of Eastern and Southern Europeans to England, and an inflow from the empire itself began to take shape. Immigrants of that era were met with the expectation to integrate into the host culture.

It was not, however, until the age of decolonization and the collapse of the empire, especially in the 1970s, that large-scale immigration from South Asia accelerated, bringing a significant Muslim community to England, with different languages, values, and cultures. In order to describe the cultural transition underway in the UK, an interpretive model refined in the United States was imported: the older notion of a singular (or nearly singular) British identity gave way to programs of multiculturalism, which emphasize the value of alternative and diverse traditions but, at the same time, tend to lock immigrant populations into the identity politics of their cultural difference. Instead of guiding immigrants on a path toward assimilation into a host culture, multiculturalism posited separate cultural zones: the host culture should adapt to the immigrants. Diversity became destiny, a mandate to refuse a shared culture of national identity and equal citizenship. To understand the UK's response to Islamist terrorism, it is crucial to keep this multicultural transformation of Britain in mind. At stake is less a national community secured by a sense of common culture and comprehensive solidarity than a weakened fabric of diverse subcultures. The legacy of the erstwhile national culture became burdened with a politically correct sense of a guilty colonial past—although it is at times, paradoxically, precisely sectors of the immigrant community, aspiring to upward mobility, who hold most firmly to the promises of modernity.

The first large wave of Muslim immigration headed to England's industrial north, driven by economic concerns and searching for jobs. The religion that these early immigrants brought with them was often worn lightly, more a set of traditionalist cultural practices than a dogmatic creed. However, the 1980s brought profound changes and politicization. The Western alliance with the anti-Communist mujahadeen opposed to the Russian occupation of Afghanistan opened up a flow of "Afghan fighters"—often as not, Arab (rather than native Afghan) veterans of the war, who carried with them a radical doctrine of jihad and Islamist transformation. Despite the East-West divide of the Cold War, their antipathy to Soviet Communism mutated with surprising ease into a symmetrical animosity toward Western consumer societies. Of course, this was not self-evident: one could imagine that these veteran activists might have settled in the West on the basis of their visceral anti-Communism, just as anti-Communist refugees from Eastern Europe and Cuba had done in the past. In this case, however, a new dynamic came into play. From the Islamist point of view, Communism and Western capitalism seemed to be variants of a fundamentally contemptible secular modernity, incompatible with the pursuit of an Islamist order.

This latent disdain for the West exploded into the public eye in the dispute over the publication of celebrated author Salman Rushdie's novel, *The Satanic Verses,* in 1988. Rushdie, an Indian-born Muslim but long a resident of London, had woven a complex tapestry in his novel: in part an account of the travails of immigration between Bombay and London, in part a meditation on the origins of Islam, and in part a parody of the sacred asceticism and cruelty of religious fervor, for many readers clearly a polemical attack on the Ayatollah Khomeini and the Islamic Revolution that had seized power in Iran in 1979. Khomeini returned the favor by denouncing the book's treatment of Mohammed and issuing a fatwa, a religious-legal order calling for Rushdie's assassination.

This affair, in which Western governments and publishers proved to be less than stalwart defenders of freedom of expression, lay the groundwork for other clashes of civilization that would play out between radical Islam and the West in the following decades (for example, the Danish Mohammed cartoons in 2005 or the response to Pope Benedict's Regensburg speech in 2006). In British cities, volumes of *The Satanic Verses* were burned in public by crowds of demonstrators. Some bookstores refrained from stocking it—but others, standing on principle, bravely did. Some public figures denounced the novel—but others defended the freedom of expression. A line in the sand had been drawn between the value of literary freedom, on the one hand, and the multicultural insistence on respect for diverse traditions, on the other. While the Rushdie affair therefore raised questions about the texture of a free society, especially the relative value of artistic freedom and tolerance for religious difference—a tension at the very heart of Western modernity—it also made clear how a radicalization of Islam was beginning to spread, transforming Britain's Muslim communities. The protesters and book-burners were not merely the small cohort of former Afghan fighters or the Islamist ideologues but drew from much larger swaths of the immigrant population.

The development of a radical Islamist element within the larger British Muslim community continued during the 1990s, especially in the wake of the collapse of the former Yugoslavia and the wars in the Balkans. Afghan fighters sometimes made their way to the West after participating in the fighting in Bosnia. The fact that the West was engaged in explicit efforts to protect the Muslims of Bosnia did little to moderate the Islamist rejection of Western modernity. The jihadist agenda, which had once been directed against the Soviet Communist occupation of Afghanistan, quickly transformed into a program for pan-Islamic solidarity with the victims in Bosnia, Chechnya, Kashmir, Palestine, and eventually in Iraq and (again) in Afghanistan—and this solidarity implied a rejectionist agenda toward the West, including those societies in which Muslim immigrants had found their new homes. Throughout Europe, some mosques and Islamic centers became focal points for Islamist polemic and the recruitment of new participants in the violent struggle. On the one hand, it is crucial to distinguish between this radical core, hostile to their host environments, and the large majority of immigrants who—despite some alienation, discrimination, and marginalization—display considerable loyalty to their new homes. On the other hand, radical activists could find some protection and cover within the larger community, which offered a constant supply of disgruntled youth, for whom jihad could seem an attractive alternative identity as a heroic warrior, surely a more glamorous and romantic prospect than unemployment or marginalization through the condescension of multiculturalism. The unique complexity of this cultural profile involves the fact that this rejectionist attitude toward England could

coexist side by side with participation in the practices and
rituals of British culture—some of the London bombers
played soccer and cricket. The London bombers acted out of
a mixture of pan-Islamic solidarity, in a protest against British
foreign policy, and contempt for Western modernity. Yet
many members of the same immigrant community from which
they emerged appreciated the opportunities for integration and
upward mobility that British society promised them, whether
or not the promise was likely to be fulfilled. For all the Islamist radicalism that incubates in immigrant communities, there
is also an important strain of immigrant optimism that aspires
for success.

One of the most resonant expressions of this immigrant
optimism is Monica Ali's 2003 novel, *Brick Lane.* Born in
Bangladesh in 1967, Ali came with her family to England at
the age of three, eventually attending Oxford. *Brick Lane,* her
first novel, was shortlisted for the prestigious Booker Prize.
In it she recounts the story of Nazneen, a Bangladeshi village
girl who is sent to London to marry Chanu, a man twice her
age, living in Brick Lane, the main street in the Bangladeshi
area of London. The novel provides a variegated account of
intertwining immigrant lives. Chanu prides himself on his familiarity with canonic British culture and aspires to assimilation but maintains the patriarchal authority of a traditionalist
family life at home. He is, however, compelled to borrow
money, which Nazneen must pay back to an unsavory figure,
polemically named Mrs. Islam, who hypocritically works
around the Muslim injunction against taking interest on debts.
Meanwhile, Nazneen falls for a handsome young man, Karim,
who introduces her to the world of Islamic political activism.
Karim combines a rhetoric of political rebellion with an expectation that Nazneen remain a modest village girl. Through-

out the novel, Nazneen exchanges letters with her sister in Bangladesh, providing a constant counterpoint to life in London. The crux of the immigrant experience, then, is the perpetual tug-of-war between traditionalist cultural structures and the opportunities for change and improvement. In the end, when Chanu, the immigrant who never succeeds, decides to return home, Nazneen refuses to accompany him; she chooses instead to stay in London with their two daughters. For the novel has been, ultimately, her story, her voyage from the South Asian village to the British metropolis. We see her at the beginning, venturing out into a city where she feels invisible and with barely two words of English, but by the conclusion, she has found the self-confidence to act on her own. She gradually encounters the opportunities this new life can afford her. As her daughter encourages her in the final words of the novel, "This is England. . . . You can do whatever you like."

Ali's endorsement of the benefits of immigration to England focuses on the greater freedom of the individual: Nazneen, who had originally been sent into an arranged marriage, ends up an independent woman with emerging business opportunities. This liberalism, however, has gone hand in hand with critiques of traditionalism and religion, which contributed to a controversy that erupted in 2006 around the filming of the novel. Activist groups around Brick Lane objected to the portrayal of the local community, and this dispute was magnified by a cultural altercation between two leading writers. Feminist author Germaine Greer adopted the multicultural position of defending the community at all costs: "Ali did not concern herself with the possibility that her plot might seem outlandish to the people who created the particular culture of Brick Lane. . . . The community has the moral right to keep the filmmakers out." A profound flaw in Greer's account, however, is that it was only some members of the Brick Lane community who opposed the film. This is the Achilles' heel of all multiculturalism: how to determine which specific representatives can credibly speak for a minority group. Even more important is Greer's worrisome assumption that any community groups—even in a case where one could demonstrate genuinely widespread support—should have the authority to place limits on an individual's freedom of speech or artistic expression. The controversy grew when *Satanic Verses* author Salman Rushdie sided with Ali and recalled that Greer had also refused to support him some fifteen years earlier when he faced the death threat of Khomeini's fatwa.

No doubt, one might well dismiss this debate over the filming of the novel as a tempest in the British literary teapot—Greer and Rushdie had attended university together and were long-standing acquaintances and adversaries. Yet the matter does have an important symptomatic standing. On the side of individual and artistic freedom stand two Muslim immigrants, Ali and Rushdie, fully integrated into the culture of Western modernity and critical of repressive traditions. Stalwart defenders of individual rights, they face simultaneous resistance from multiple quarters—from both immigrant community organizers (the self-appointed guardians of the Brick Lane community who attack the freedom of artistic representation) and from the elite defenders of liberal multiculturalism. One might have thought that Greer, a pioneer of literary feminism, might have sided with Ali, whose novel after all celebrates the emancipation narrative of a heroine who learns to stand on her own two feet. Yet the multicultural turn in the progressive political community has tended to undermine appreciation for the value of individual freedom and to subordinate it to community values, frequently defined in repressive terms. This has taken a particular toll on feminism: where community values and women's rights collide, it is nearly always women who have to give ground in the name of protecting cultural diversity. This repressive aspect of multiculturalism has been crucial for the discussion of Islam in Britain as part of the response to terrorism, and the center of the storm has been at the intersection of religion and law with regard to the status of sharia, traditional Muslim jurisprudence.

On February 7, 2008, the Archbishop of Canterbury, Rowan Williams, delivered a lecture entitled "Civil and Religious Law in England: a Religious Perspective" at the Royal Courts of Justice, the inaugural address of a series on Islam and English Law. His speech concerned the status of law in a society in which individuals increasingly hold multiple affiliations—a multicultural society—and the pressures that this restructuring places on conventional post-enlightenment claims for universality and equality. In the course of the argument he explores the possible role for sharia within a British legal framework. Understanding how controversial a topic he is broaching, Williams takes pains to indicate that he is excluding "committed Islamic primitivists"—that is, Salafist proponents of a return to an original Muslim social order, whom he distinguishes as extremists from the mainstream of Islamic legal thinking. In addition, Williams insists that nothing he proposes should limit anyone's access to essential human rights. Given those qualifications, Williams undertakes to explore how sharia might play a positive role in Britain.

Williams's claims unleashed a firestorm of criticism, particularly because in a BBC radio interview he appeared to endorse the notion that sharia was "unavoidable." The complexity and nuance of his speech disappeared in some of the public reporting, as other church leaders, including his pre-decessor, Lord Carey, and the Pakistan-born Michael Nazir-Ali, the Bishop of Rochester, called for his resignation. Yet this was not simply a matter of journalistic sensationalism, as some of Williams's defenders suggested. At stake was the highly sensitive question of the modification of law in the age of multiculturalism. If, as Williams argued, contemporary identity often involved multiple affiliations, it could be pos-sible that members of certain communities might find alter-native legal orders more credible. Minimally, this might be treated as a defense of religious courts to adjudicate certain limited matters on a voluntary basis for members of a faith, often concerning marriage and divorce. Yet the implication of Williams's statement was in fact much larger. In the words of one commentator, "a growing number of people (Muslims and others) feel that they have no stake in British society, its institutions and its values. The resulting social meltdown is reflected in a crisis in our legal system. . . . This breakdown in trust, law, and social cohesion has a particularly devastating impact upon young people." From this point of view, the en-tire legal order suffers from a legitimation deficit, and espe-cially so in immigrant communities.

Williams's proposal basically involved modifying the post-enlightenment model of uniform justice—one law for everyone—by allowing for variation appropriate to a soci-ety of diverse allegiances: different laws for different com-munities. Yet his position is more complex. The interest in diversity is the flipside of a conservative anxiety about the consequences of an extremist pursuit of equality: "Where [ab-stract citizenship] has been enforced, it has proved a weak vehicle for the life of a society and has often brought violent injustice in its wake (think of the various attempts to reduce citizenship to rational equality in the France of the 1790s or the China of the 1970s)." For Williams, the issue is not that immigration produced a cultural diversity that undermined some previously functioning universalism. Rather, the very program of abstract universalism was insufficient from the start. There is more to social life than abstract law, or, in his words, "the important springs of moral vision in a society will be in those areas which a systematic abstract universalism regards as 'private'—in religion above all, but also in custom and habit." Here, interestingly enough, Williams' contemplation of the potential role of sharia betrays a conservative predisposition in his claim that binding values are more likely to emerge from the private sphere, the world of religion and tradition, than from the mechanical legality of the state.

To countenance the introduction of sharia seems, for some, a catastrophic opening to the sort of extremism associated with the Taliban or Wahabi Islam. While Williams explicitly excludes those versions by rejecting "primitivism," wise critics remain skeptical of his proposition, since he is, in effect, calling for a modification of the principle of equal justice for all. Yet even if one could exclude the extremist variation, the prospect of sharia appears to contribute to the further balkanization of society into multicultural enclaves, while blurring the border between state and religion. That recourse to religion, however, is precisely what makes sharia attractive to Williams. For the Archbishop of Canterbury, contemporary society needs more religious presence, not less. In his proposal, therefore, he does not speak as a Christian objecting to aspects of Islam (as did, for example, Benedict XVI in his Regensburg address of 2006). Instead he speaks as a proponent of the importance of any (non-extremist) religious affiliation as a salutary addition to the complexity of contem-

porary identities. Religion—even a non-Christian religion—
can help heal the wounds of a secular and excessively abstract
society.

Williams contemplated the introduction of sharia courts
on the basis of voluntary compliance. Since his address, a
more robust institutionalization has however taken place on
the basis of the Arbitration Act of 1996: if the parties to a
dispute agree to accept a sharia court as an arbitration tribunal,
its rulings become enforceable through the power of the British judicial system. In other words, once the arbitration begins, the outcome becomes binding with the full force of law.
As of September 2008, five such tribunals were in place—in
London, Birmingham, Bradford, Manchester, and Nuneaton,
Warwickshire—with plans for more in Glasgow and Edin-
burgh. (The Jewish court system of the Beth Din operates on
the same legal basis.) Cases have included Muslim divorce,
inheritance adjudications, and disputes with neighbors. Sheikh
Faiz-ul-Aqtab Siddiqi, chairman of the Governing Council
of the Muslim Arbitration Tribunal, the organization that
manages the courts, has commented that they will handle
"smaller" criminal cases: "All we are doing is regulating community affairs." If such tribunals have greater credibility
within the Muslim community than does the regular court system, is that not the advantage Williams sought? Nonetheless
there are critics, including prominent Conservative politician
Dominic Grieve, who complained, "If it is true that these tribunals are passing binding decisions in the areas of family
and criminal law, I would like to know which courts are en-
forcing them because I would consider such action unlawful.
British law is absolute and must remain so." Yet it was precisely the absoluteness of universal law that Williams identified as the source of the problem. Williams also hoped that

an alternative court system would not lead to a reduction of individual rights. According to the *Times,* however, some rulings of the sharia courts appear to have been worrisomely at odds with standard British justice, advantaging sons over daughters in inheritance disputes and minimizing the consequences of domestic violence.

Scapegoats

The British response to Islamist terrorism has, as we have seen, involved vigorous debates. In terms of security legislation, strong cases have been mounted for enhanced police powers as well as against them, in order to defend legal traditions and human rights. Because of the scope of immigration and because of the perception of "homegrown terrorism" on 7/7, the response has also involved an introspection regarding the character of contemporary British society and culture: should it differentiate into multicultural enclaves in order to accommodate alternative traditions and sensibilities or should it insist on core values and a unified legal system? These are complex matters that do not lend themselves to simplistic answers. There is, however, a third dimension to the British response that has a different character, a search for a culprit to blame for the terrorist violence. It could be worth pondering why it is so difficult to blame the perpetrators themselves, those who carry out the bombings and the ideologues who recruited them. Yet that sort of clear indictment is often elusive; instead the search for a scapegoat commences, leading to two standard outcomes: Americans and Jews.

Firstly, for significant parts of the opinion-making classes, blame falls squarely on the shoulders of the United States and its leadership during the Bush administration. They tout the untenable argument that American foreign policy is the source of all evil in the world and, without it, no Islamist terrorism would take place. The name for this sort of blanket condemnation of the United States is anti-Americanism, described lucidly by acclaimed novelist Margaret Drabble in a memorable essay of 2003: "My anti-Americanism has become almost uncontrollable. It has possessed me, like a disease. It rises up in my throat like acid reflux, that fashionable American sickness. I now loathe the United States and what it has done to Iraq and the rest of the helpless world. . . . I detest Disneyfication, I detest Coca-Cola, I detest burgers, I detest sentimental and violent Hollywood movies that tell lies about history, I detest American imperialism, American infantilism, and American triumphalism about victories it didn't even win."

Drabble is gratefully unambiguous in her confession of anti-Americanism, if, unfortunately, not ironic. Policy disputes based on rational argument do not add up to anti-Americanism, but this sort of irrational rage clearly demonstrates how affect can displace reason. During the Bush years, anti-Americanism of this ilk generated extraordinary tensions in transatlantic relations, although significantly less between the United States and England than between the United States and France and Germany. The most egregious expressions of anti-Americanism began to wane fairly early during President Bush's second term and have dwindled significantly since President Obama took office, although this change in sentiment has yet to lead to any concrete results, such as noteworthy changes in European participation in shared foreign policy initiatives.

While anti-Americanism was somewhat less of an issue in England than in continental Europe, a second scapegoating has taken on extraordinary proportions: British anti-Semitism.

The ideological fusion of anti-Americanism and anti-Semitism has a history stretching back into the nineteenth century, and it has become virulent in extremist circles today. Yet what characterizes aspects of British political culture in the age of Islamist terrorism is a peculiarly tenacious vilification of Jews and Israel. To be sure, critique of Israeli policies is not in and of itself anti-Semitic—Israelis criticize their governments constantly, and Israeli policies are hardly beyond reproach. Yet what is equally clear, consistent, and extreme anti-Zionism regularly goes hand in hand with anti-Semitism. The argument, increasingly common in England, that the existence of the State of Israel is the root cause of Islamist terrorism, is regularly intertwined with anti-Semitic opinion. This is all the more the case at this historical moment when a major regional power, Iran, has threatened to eradicate Israel; however, what concerns us here is how the response to Islamist terrorism in England has counterintuitively turned toward the terminologies and imagery of anti-Semitism.

This anti-Semitic turn has marred British politics and culture throughout the decade, a bizarre shifting of attention away from Islamist terrorism. In January 2002, only four months after the attacks of 9/11, the prestigious journal *New Statesman* featured a cover infamously depicting a golden Star of David stabbing a Union Jack with the inflammatory title "A Kosher Conspiracy?" The key articles concerned support for Israel in the media and politics, but the journal chose to illustrate them with an ominous combination of iconography (the star) and word choice (kosher) that inculpated Jews and Judaism in general. Faced with extensive protest, the journal editor, Peter Wilby, reluctantly offered an apology and a concession: "The cover was not intended to be anti-Semitic, the *New Statesman* is vigorously opposed to racism in all its forms. But it used images and words in such a way as to create unwittingly the impression that the *New Statesman* was following an anti-Semitic tradition that sees the Jews as a conspiracy piercing the heart of the nation." Indeed it was doing so in the context of the emergence, on both sides of the Atlantic, of the highly charged accusation that "neocons," a term used increasingly as a code for politically conservative Jews, were engaged in a "cabal" (another term with an innuendo of a Jewish conspiracy) to manipulate Western foreign policy. A strange new perspective was emerging: the enemy ceased to be the perpetrators of 9/11 but the advocates of a preventive strategy against future assaults. Because Islamists had attacked the West, Jews became suspect.

After the *New Statesman* affair, anti-Semitic imagery returned to British political debate soon enough. In the run-up to the 2005 elections, the Labor Party denounced the Conservative program to reduce taxes and to limit spending with a poster showing two pigs with wings and with the heads of two prominent Conservatives—Michael Howard, the party leader, and Oliver Letwin, the shadow Chancellor of the Exchequer—whose policies will work, presumably, when pigs fly. Both Howard and Letwin are Jewish. A second poster followed quickly: Michael Howard cast as Fagin, the anti-Semitic stereotype from Charles Dickens's novel *Oliver Twist*, drawing on an image from the popular musical *Oliver!* In response to protests against the anti-Semitic innuendoes, the posters were withdrawn, but the message was clear. In England, caricaturing Jews is more amusing than confronting Islamists.

There are no obvious grounds to assume genuine ideological anti-Semitism in the Labor Party leadership, but something else was evidently at stake. Several weeks after the poster controversies, the British minister of trade, Mike O'Brien, wrote in *The Muslim Weekly* that Muslims should not trust Howard. While he did not mention that Howard is Jewish, he could, after all, assume that was common knowledge, especially in the wake of the poster campaigns. Yet when he also cautioned the Muslim readership against the Liberal Democrats, he chose not to mention that party's leader but instead revealingly singled out a much less prominent figure, Evan Harris, the sole Jewish member of the senior Liberal Democrat parliamentary group. It is impossible to resist the conclusion that part of the Labor campaign strategy involved playing on anti-Semitic predispositions, perhaps especially (although by no means exclusively) in the Muslim population. As Jonathan Rosenblum has argued, "The party has done the math, and it does not augur well for the Jews. There are less than 300,000 identifying Jews in England today, and over six times as many Moslems. The road to electoral success lies in appeasing Moslem voters. To that end, the Labor Party did not hesitate to remind voters in the last election of the Jewish origins of Conservative Party chairman Michael Howard."

The spread of anti-Semitism in England has not been limited to the world of journalism and politics. Since as early as 2002, British universities have been at the center of a movement to boycott Israeli universities. On April 22, 2005, the Council of Association of University Teachers voted to boycott Bar-Ilan University because it offered courses in the West Bank, and Haifa University because it had disciplined a lecturer involved with a student's falsification of evidence. Criticisms of the vote—which had been scheduled to conflict with a Jewish holiday—were vocal, including from the Palestinian president of Al-Quds University, Sari Nusseibeh. Through an extraordinary petition process, a special meeting was called at

which the boycott was cancelled. Nonetheless, calls for boy-
cotts continue, both of Israeli universities and of individual
Israeli academics who do not adequately criticize their government. On January 16, 2009, an open letter in the *Guardian*,
signed by numerous British academics, again called for boy-
cotts. Jewish groups have denounced such appeals as anti-
Semitic, and they have been widely deplored in the United
States. While the boycott campaign has had some small
resonance internationally, it remains largely a British phenomenon. Although academics face censorship and political
restrictions in many countries, including the Arab world,
British university faculty have focused exclusively on a boycott of Israel.

The proliferation of anti-Semitism in the UK has become
such a matter of public concern that a Parliamentary Committee against Anti-Semitism has been formed, and it has issued an extensive report. In fact, the level of anti-Semitism
in the UK is on the low end of opinions found elsewhere in
Europe, according to a 2009 report by the Anti-Defamation
League, and England appears to be the only country where
levels of anti-Semitism have declined since a 2007 survey.
Yet a decline late in the decade is also indicative of a peak
in the middle of the period under discussion here. Particularly
in the cultural sphere, theatrical performances that interweave
anti-Semitism and anti-Zionism, whether through one-sided
criticism of Israel or through mobilizations of anti-Semitic
images, have been staged repeatedly in London, to some ac-
claim and always with controversy. Just as the expansion of
antiterror legislation elicited debate between proponents and
opponents, so too has this spread of anti-Semitism on the British stage.

Given an increasing hesitation across the continent to publish works or display artwork that can be read as critical of Islam, it is noteworthy how eagerly the stage has lent itself to the production of anti-Israel performances. Foremost among these is the play *My Name Is Rachel Corrie,* which draws from the diaries and correspondence of a young American member of the radical International Solidarity Movement. Corrie had traveled to the Gaza Strip and, in the course of a protest demonstration against the destruction of guerilla hideouts, she was killed by a bulldozer operated by the Israeli Defense Forces. Although the Israelis claim the death was accidental, Corrie became an iconic martyr for the anti-Israel movement. Her writings were edited and staged first in April 2005 at the Royal Court Theater. Many positive reviews praised the play for the portrayal of Corrie's passion; others denounced its distortions. Commenting on Corrie's characterization of the Palestinians as "engaging in Gandhian nonviolent resistance," the reviewer for the *Times,* Clive Davis, wrote that "even the late Yassir Arafat might have blushed at that one." Given its success on the London stage, the play has since been performed around the world. Some critics have objected to its propagandistic character. Reviewing a Vancouver performance, Peter Birnie wrote: "An excellent piece of polemic, *My Name is Rachel Corrie* is a powerful slap at the state of Israel. . . . Fine. Okay. But can we please see a companion piece of theatre about a certain desert-kingdom royal family and its deep complicity in fomenting terrorism against, among many others, Israel and the world's Jewish communities? Let's call it *My Name Is Osama bin Laden.*"

Corrie has also been celebrated in a cantata by the American composer Philip Munger, *The Skies Are Weeping.* After public controversy and complaints about the anti-Semitic character of the libretto, a planned premiere at the University of Alaska in Anchorage was cancelled, but the work found a welcome reception in, not surprisingly, London, at the Hackney Empire Theater, where it opened in November 2005. Its patrons included prominent anti-Israel celebrities such as Noam Chomsky and Ilan Pappé, with support from many and sundry anti-Zionist organizations. More influential, however, has been another play by celebrated British playwright Caryl Churchill, *Seven Jewish Children,* first performed at the Royal Court Theater in February 2009. In this brief, ten-minute litany, adult voices discuss what to tell, and what not tell a child about the history of Israel. At stake ultimately is a venomous caricature of Jewish and Israeli identity, especially through Churchill's imputation of sentiments of unmitigated brutality to some of the Israeli voices. While anti-Zionist critics have rallied to the play, it was described in *The Sunday Times* as "straitjacketed political orthodoxy," and critic Melanie Philips has called it "an open vilification of the Jewish people . . . drawing upon an atavistic hatred of the Jews" and an "open incitement to hatred." Efforts to defend the play on its artistic merits and to ward off political criticisms have been undercut by Churchill's own decision to make the transcript of the play accessible to all without charge, as long as performances generate fund-raising for Gaza.

It is possible to debate the political aesthetics of these works—*My Name Is Rachel Corrie, The Skies Are Weeping,* and *Seven Jewish Children.* What is indisputable, however, is the proliferation of stridently anti-Israel productions on the London stage. Evidently there is a welcoming public for radical anti-Zionism in England, especially when it spills over into anti-Semitism. This sets London apart from other European capitals. While it is clear that anti-Semitic sentiments thrive elsewhere, as the ADL study has demonstrated, they are nowhere so much a central piece of high culture as in England. To trace the complex genealogy of British anti-Semitism would lead far beyond the scope of this chapter. Suffice it to conclude here that among the multifaceted English responses to Islamist terrorism, one of the most enigmatic is this sudden resurgence of an elite anti-Semitism. Suicide bombers attacked the London Underground in the name of Islam, and the response of the British stage has been to pillory Jews. The trauma of 7/7 needed a scapegoat, and theater found a very traditional solution.

CHAPTER THREE

France

Terrorism and
the Republic

Unlike England and Spain, France has not experienced a major jihadist attack in the years since 9/11—at least not as of this writing. Nothing like the 2004 Madrid train bombing or the 2005 explosions in the London Underground has defined French political debate. To be sure, memories of an older terrorism, during the Algerian war of the 1950s and, more recently, spilling over from the Middle East in the 1980s or Algeria's own civil strife in the 1990s, linger on. Still, there has been no prominent assassination comparable to the stabbing of Theo van Gogh in the streets of Amsterdam, and although the French ban on headscarves in 2004 led to considerable public controversy, it never elicited the level of international violence that followed upon the 2005 publication of the Mohammed caricatures in Denmark: French embassies have not been targeted, French products have not been boycotted. France has not been compelled to rally around its flag, nor has it succumbed to terrorist extortion. It might seem then that France has been able to stand apart from the worst excesses of the current wave of Islamist terrorism. The French response therefore primarily involves its reactions to attacks that have taken place elsewhere, most notably 9/11. This particular perspective implies the priority of the international dimension: France addresses Islamist terrorism in terms of its own national ambitions within the international system.

Nonetheless, and perhaps paradoxically, in no other country has the concern with terrorism and a generalized loss of a sense of domestic security grown as pronounced as in France. Despite the absence of a major terrorist attack in France, anxieties about terrorism have merged seamlessly with worries about a breakdown of law and order in the streets, intertwined with rampant fears about the social disorder associated with the *banlieues*: the suburbs and satellite cities that surround France's urban centers, which have become concentrated sites of restive immigrant populations. In the autumn of 2005, civil unrest spread across France, initially in response to the accidental death of two teenagers in Clichy-sous-Bois, just east of Paris, but the rioting cascaded rapidly across the country, drawing especially on the North African and Muslim immigrant populations. The government declared a state of emergency that lasted three months: property losses were estimated at 200 million euros, and nearly three thousand rioters were arrested. Another wave of riots took place in the summer of 2009: high unemployment surely played a role, just as the experience of perceived discrimination elicited resentment, but a more general alienation from French society on the part of immigrant youth—the feeling that one's prospects of entering the mainstream of French life are very limited—was exacerbated by the spread of extremist Islamist ideology. This is the explosive point where dissatisfaction with social conditions, leading to a sense of despair, can intersect with the noxious contents of radical ideology. As long as that dissatisfaction festers, radicalism can remain tempting. Islamism in particular provides a language to the resentment that, initially, may not be religious at all, but the result is no less dangerous. France sits on a tinderbox, and its conflicted responses to terrorism are driven by alternative hopes: to achieve a modicum of security, while trying to avoid antagonizing the domestic Muslim population in the *banlieues* and pursuing a long-standing national foreign policy agenda of opening toward the Arab world.

This distinctiveness of the French response to terrorism derives from its own national cultural traditions and the institutions that set it apart from its European neighbors. In all countries, some elements of the historical past define the terrain within which contemporary policies are formulated, but that weight of the past works in different ways. In Germany, the past appears as a burdensome legacy obligating today's generations to avoid replicating the crimes of their predecessors: the German discussions about counterterrorism or immigrant assimilation are complex and diverse but ultimately a function of national memories of the Nazi era. In contrast to these German efforts to escape its past, England inherits the legacy of empire by (generally) embracing a metropolitan diversity, just as it cultivates a pronounced tradition of civil liberties: these two strands define responses to Islamism and the Muslim world. For England much depends on a balancing act between individual rights and group discourses on multiculturalism. France too has a history of empire, and with it comes some sense of guilt and remorse, but the French national past remains, by and large, a set of positive contents that produce a symptomatic package of political concerns: the legacy of the French Revolution and, especially, the Third

Republic combine to make up a republican political culture
with a widely shared and deeply internalized commitment to
core civic values: the rule of law, the civil rights of individuals, emphatic secularism (*laïcité,* or "laicism"), and a profound commitment to French national identity—that is, to the
values of the republic—as well as to French national interest.

This modernized nationalism is not uniquely French, although it has a particular prominence there. Contemporary
German nationalism is refracted through the very powerful
federalist institutions, which in turn intentionally limit the
power of the national government and its ability to command
an exclusive loyalty. Britain, with its royal household, does
retain, perhaps enigmatically, sets of traditions, including a
relative prominence to the role of religious faith in public life.
In contrast, in France, a sense of centralized and uniformly
shared national identity, including an obligation to a strong
state, forms the basis of political discourse, and it is from this
vantage point that both Islamist terrorism and Muslim integration are viewed and interpreted. Of course, the various European nations face very similar challenges: how to grapple
with the complex interface of Islamist terrorist networks and
large Muslim immigrant populations. Yet while Germany approaches these matters in the shadow of its national past, anx-
ious about privacy rights and the rule of law; and while the
UK focuses on the multicultural legacy of empire and the
diversity of traditions, France places primary emphasis on the
integrity of the national republic. A peculiar set of responses,
direct and indirect, to Islamist terrorism ensues, including a
focus on the status of France in the international system, the
specifically robust character of counterterrorism measures, and
expectations of egalitarianism, deriving from a long-standing

sense of civic membership. Yet a surprising companion to that civic egalitarianism has been, on occasion, a fascination with terrorists, precisely as embodiments of an alternative politics. This romanticization and sometimes celebration of the violent political actor as a noble savage stands at odds with the strength of French counterterrorist policing efforts. The French reaction to Islamist terrorism in the post–9/11 world includes all these various elements, reflecting both the complexity of French society, culture, and politics, as well as the complicated texture of politicized and violent Islamism.

The Grand Nation in the International System

To understand the French concerns with terrorism, we also have to explore why America's oldest ally became the epicenter of anti-Americanism during the Iraq war. That opposition stood out in bold contrast to the initial response to 9/11. The day after the Al Qaeda attacks in New York and Washington, the leading French daily, *Le Monde*, famously proclaimed that "We are all Americans now," a brave declaration of solidarity with the United States facing Islamist terrorism. Yet it quickly became apparent that that identification with the victim did not at all imply solidarity in the response that the U.S. government chose. *Le Monde* could offer symbolic allegiance, but France was much more hesitant about the foreign policy consequences.

In the highly partisan American debates since 2001, a standard account has developed, attributing this shift in the French position to the so-called unilateralism of the Bush administration. Indeed, the argument is made not only concerning France but all of "old Europe," in Donald Rumsfeld's phrase, or even world opinion in general. Yet we know that even in the immediate aftermath of 9/11, there were significant minorities in Europe that opposed any American response. More specifically, however, political dynamics within Europe, and especially within France, were bound to place very real and practical limits on the seemingly unlimited expression of verbal support: talk is cheap.

Some blame can certainly be placed on Jacques Chirac's political opportunism: he could secure his position in the competitive world of French politics by leveraging his personal opposition to the politics associated with George W. Bush. In effect, he could run "against Washington," even in his campaign for the presidency of France. Yet this strategy to draw on strains of anti-Americanism in the French electorate was not merely a card to play in electoral campaigns. It also reflected deep-seated concerns about the status of France in the international system and its efforts to remain an important player in international politics, even as its significance was objectively declining. Indeed, France's status as a world power had been dwindling at least since the First World War (if not longer), and this development only accelerated after the end of the Cold War and German unification. Nonetheless, France has remained adamantly jealous of maintaining its independent voice in international affairs. This French national ambition structured parts of its response to terrorism. Solidarity with America under attack—which may well have been sincere and could certainly build on a long-standing alliance—was not about to cancel the French national agenda. International rejection of Islamist terrorism does not erase distinct national interests: French maneuvering in the wake of 9/11 demonstrates the durability of interest differences even in the face of the apparent threat of terrorism and the state of emergency it has tended to elicit.

The end of the Cold War diminished the French position in international affairs. The end of the division of Europe meant that Western Europe ceased to be the privileged front-line of the decades-old standoff between the U.S. and the USSR. Of course, American foreign policy since then remains engaged in Europe, but the significance of other parts of the world, in particular transpacific affairs, has grown ever more apparent. Even within the American elite, decades of criticism of "Eurocentrism" have taken their toll, further undermining a traditional orientation to Europe. This tectonic shift may have been moderated in the UK due to a long-standing special relationship among the Anglophone powers. France, in addition, had (like England) resisted the unification of Germany, which, after the fall of the Berlin Wall, emerged as the leading continental power, not only due to its size and population but to its enhanced opportunities in Central and Eastern Europe. While France could see its position within Europe threatened by its newly whole neighbor to the east, Europe in general suffered a blow to its prestige by its inability to respond effectively to the crises that followed from the collapse of Yugoslavia (as discussed in Chapter Six on Bosnia). Even in "its own backyard," Europe proved ineffective and had to rely on American strength.

In this rapidly shifting context that challenged France's stature, a robust pursuit of French national interests became especially urgent, and the Bush administration's response to 9/11 provided Chirac with an opportunity to profile France (and himself) in international affairs. What became, in popular political culture, a wave of anti-Americanism, was a consequence of Chirac's efforts to assert French leadership in an era in which it had lost much of its meaning. Viewed from this point of view, it was a classically conservative foreign policy, an effort to assert national interests and identity at an opportune moment. It should also not be forgotten that in this post–9/11 period, French political leadership has been consistently conservative—in contrast to the primacy of the Labor Party in the UK and the shifting coalitions in Germany, which, until 2009, included the center-left Social Democrats. If France played the role of the key antagonist to the American response to Islamist terrorism, it did so through conservative political leaders. This political coding of the French response to Islamism has continued into the Sarkozy government. Despite the considerable personal enmity between Chirac and Sarkozy, and despite Sarkozy's pro-American image, he has emphatically endorsed, in retrospect, Chirac's resistance of the Iraq war: "Everyone knows of your determining role in the Iraq affair of 2003. You saw things correctly," Sarkozy praised his predecessor on November 6, 2009, at a ceremony in Paris. It is hard to imagine a clearer demonstration of continuity in the elite articulation of a French national foreign policy. As much as the tone of French relations to Washington has changed with the shift from Chirac to Sarkozy, fundamental aspects of French national interests remain constant.

A related factor pertinent to the French response to Islamist terrorism involves the historic foreign policy agenda of building transmediterranean connections to the Arab world. At least since the era of Charles de Gaulle, France has attempted to become the west European country that could serve as a bridge to North Africa. In some ways, these ambitions toward the Arab region represented a transformation of the long history of French colonialism. The nineteenth-century efforts to incorporate the southern shore of the Mediterranean into a French empire turned into a systematic courting of the postcolonial regimes. This particular dimension of foreign policy made France even more predisposed to avoid any direct criticisms of Islam. It also proved conducive to an extensive flow of immigration from Muslim Africa into the French urban centers. This complex interaction between France and the Arab world has tended to make French leadership cautious and indeed reluctant to criticize Islamist radicalism: too much has been invested in constructing the relationship with Muslim countries to let it be jeopardized by a polemic against Islamist extremists. Needless to say, the result did not at all imply any condoning, let alone endorsement of terrorism, but it did mitigate against the sort of frontal ideological assault sometimes articulated during the Bush administration as part of the war on terror. In general, the result has been not only a set of policies but also a public discourse in France that has tended to be more open to pro-Arab positions than elsewhere in the West, especially the United States, and therefore more apprehensive of emphatic critiques of Islam or even Islamism. As we will see, this reluctance to criticize Islamism can coexist well with forceful counterterrorism strategies, but France has been careful not to underscore the war on Islamist terrorism in public declarations. Wielding a big stick of counterterrorism techniques, France nonetheless often walks softly.

A telling piece of evidence concerning the French public discussion (as opposed to French government policy) and its relationship to terrorism in the post–9/11 era is the curious popularity of conspiracy-theory accounts of the attacks in New York and Washington. Born in 1957, Thierry Meyssan was active in French left politics during the 1990s, focusing especially on matters of homosexual rights and the decriminalization of drugs. He gained international notoriety, however, with the 2002 publication of his book *9/11—The Big Lie,* a systematic rejection of the standard accounts of the terrorist attacks. According to Meyssan, it was not Al Qaeda under the leadership of Osama bin Laden who authored the attacks but rather a conspiracy within the U.S. government, seeking a pretext to initiate a long-planned war in Afghanistan. Indeed, for Meyssan, bin Laden was little more than an American agent in a strategy driven by the military-industrial complex and right-wing Christian extremists. Speaking at the Zayed Center in Abu Dhabi in April 2002, he asserted, "it appears that the attacks of September cannot be attributed to foreign terrorists from the Arab-Muslim world—even if some of those involved might have been Muslim—but to United States terrorists."

Meyssan's account has faced severe criticism, not only in the United States (including from government sources), but also from the mainstream and center-left press in France. Yet *9/11—The Big Lie* does have symptomatic value insofar as it remained on French bestseller lists for months, indicating a French predisposition to deny the reality of Islamist terrorism. For some significant fraction of the French population, a murderous conspiracy within the U.S. government was more plausible than the reality of a jihadist attack on the Twin Towers and the Pentagon. Still, it would be wrong to treat Meyssan's conspiracy theory as in any way typical of French responses to 9/11. On the contrary, the mainstream press largely regards him as lacking credibility and he has been banned from French television. He has, however, appeared frequently on television throughout much of the Arab world, in Iran, in Russia, and parts of Latin America (including Venezuela). He has made his home in Lebanon, where he declared his political proximity to Hezbollah and his admiration for its leader, Hassan Nasrallah. In this context, however, the point is that his fringe conspiracy theory did have extensive appeal among significant parts of the French public. It sold a lot of books.

Thus we have seen that both on the level of official foreign policy formulation and in popular political discussion, a concern with French nationhood and national interests refracts the response to 9/11. For Chirac, this meant carving out a French position opposed to Washington in order to maintain a privileged access to the Arab world—including the French involvement in the corrupt oil-for-food arrangements with Saddam Hussein's Iraq. For parts of the French reading public, the implication was the plausibility of Meyssan's extremist indictment of Washington, as a vehicle to reject accusations directed at Islamist terrorists. In both versions, attention shifted away from Islamism in order to bolster an agenda of French national sovereignty against Washington: a recapitulation of the Gaullist legacy.

However, this de facto minimalization of the Islamist threat in order to gain leverage against an American-driven war on Islamist terror reaches an objective limit when French nationality—the real goal of conservative politics—faces its own adversaries. In recent years, that threat has not materialized in the form of terrorism, in the strict sense, but rather in the waves of civil unrest that have shaken France repeatedly. A mood of insecurity, crime in the streets, and the ungovernability of the *banlieues* has given rise to a sense of cultural crisis, as if national identity were unraveling. Reminiscent of aspects of the U.S. culture wars of the 1980s, a new discussion of national identity was launched by the Sarkozy government in 2009. In fact, the topic had begun to emerge during the 2007 election campaign, and the capacity of conservatives to articulate a concern with national identity explains their ascendancy in France as much as in Germany.

The French minister of immigration, Eric Besson, called, in October 2009, for an extensive public discussion on "the theme of what it is to be French, what are the values that we share, what are the relations that make us French and of which we should be proud." It is therefore not simply a matter of determining the content of Frenchness but promoting it as a positive agenda. "We must reaffirm the values of French national identity and the pride in being French. . . . For example, I believe it would be good—this is normal in the United States, but sometimes complicated in France—for all French youth to have a chance once a year to sing the national anthem." The complication to which he refers is that the French anthem, the *Marseillaise*, has frequently been booed at soccer matches, especially where the French national team has faced teams from Algeria and Tunisia and, according to press reports, the culprits have not been foreign visitors but immigrant offspring born in France. Their gesture represents explicit rejections of the cherished symbol of official French nationality and the French republic, clear evidence of the disaffection widespread in the immigrant Muslim communities.

At the outset of the national identity debate, Besson mentioned initiatives such as civics courses for immigrants (comparable to similar educational programs in Germany). However, the move to address national identity has encountered opposition; it has been denounced as mere politics but also as an effort to dismantle multiculturalism. Yet even Sarkozy's former socialist rival, Ségolène Royal, has called on the left to engage in the nationality discussion as well, and not abandon it to the right: "The nation is originally a concept of the left. . . . We have to reconquer the symbols of the nation. That is why I wanted to have the *Marseillaise* sung at my (campaign) meetings and to reclaim the national flag that be-

longs to all of us, not just the right." Despite Royal's inter-
vention on the nationality question, most politicians on the
left have denounced the initiative as a conservative electoral
maneuver or worse. In the end, however, polls indicate that
the idea has popular support in the French population: in one
tally, 60 percent support the debate and only 35 percent oppose it; according to the sample, "French identity" is made
up of language (80 percent), the republic (64 percent), the
flag (63 percent), secularism (62 percent), and the flag (50
percent).

Like other European countries, France faces a crisis of
identity for multiple reasons, not only the growing size of
immigrant populations that seem to resist integration into
mainstream culture. The inexorable spread of the structures of
the European Union challenge historical features of national
identity, the vortex of globalization pressures the integrity of
national economies, and the reorganization of Europe in the
wake of the Cold War (and the supply of low-cost labor from
Eastern Europe) amplify social pressures, not to mention the
accelerated flow of cultural symbols in the age of the new
technologies. National identity is nowhere what it used to be.
The weakening of the bonds of national solidarity has political
implications that are complex and far-reaching in the current
process of global reorganization, and this transformation is
hardly restricted to France. France is, however, distinctive because the concept of the nation—as Royal points out—is intimately bound up with the core agenda of the republic. A
cultural policy to emphasize national values may have a conservative ring to it, but it is, in France, fundamentally tied to
deep political currents that reach back to the revolution. This
effort at a recovery of national identity is a primary aspect of
the French response to the encounter with Muslim immigra-

tion and, indirectly, it is a cultural response to the tremors of Islamist terrorism.

Counterterrorism: The French Model

The simultaneous challenges of Islamist terrorism and large-scale immigration—two distinct topics which, nonetheless, intersect when terrorist networks recruit from disaffected immigrant populations—have elicited responses in France markedly different from those elsewhere. The perceived French need to carve out a particular position in international relations and the traditional Gaullist agenda of flaunting independence from the United States have meant developing an identifiable French stance in the international war on terror. France continues to pursue its own transmediterranean opening to the Arab world, led the opposition to the Iraq war, and mounts a contingent to the war in Afghanistan that ranks in size well below those of the United States, the United Kingdom, and Germany. (Similarly, France initially resisted efforts to deploy NATO AWACS plans to support the International Security Assistance Force in Afghanistan.) While it would obviously be indefensible to depict France as avoiding participation in the international military efforts, it has not been at the forefront, lagging behind even Germany, despite that country's endemic pacifist inclinations. Meanwhile, the culture of French republicanism has led to an official policy of integrating immigrants—a policy that has dismally failed, as evidenced by the regular outbreaks of civil unrest in the immigrant ghettoes—while eschewing the programmatic multiculturalism of the United States and Britain. The coordinates of French nationalism and republicanism have contributed to these distinct paths.

Yet France has productively taken the lead in another arena, domestic counterterrorism. While crime prevention, particularly in the *banlieues,* remains a major problem and a source of deep anxiety for a public concerned with the breakdown of law and order, intelligence gathering and terror prevention have been relatively successful thanks to the development of centralized judiciary processes, coordinated intelligence, and tough legislation. This willingness to assert state power even at the cost of curtailing civil liberties represents another aspect of the republican legacy, although it has been controversial and elicited harsh criticism from the human rights community in France and abroad.

While France may have been spared post–9/11 attacks on the scale of the bombings in Madrid and London, it has, in fact, faced an extensive range of terrorist attacks dating back to the 1980s. A series of attacks on Jewish targets rattled Paris in 1980, an initial effort to put pressure on France's Middle East policies. On December 7, 1985, explosions in Parisian department stores left 45 wounded, initiating a bloody series of attacks that lasted more than a year. (Responsibility was claimed by the previously unknown Committee for Solidarity with Arab and Middle Eastern Political Prisoners, which demanded the release of several terrorist leaders then in French custody.) These attacks were linked to various conflicts in the Muslim world, and they were presumably brought to a conclusion through discreet diplomatic efforts between France and both Iran and Syria. Another wave of bombings took place in 1995 and 1996, culminating in an explosion on December 3, 1996, at the Port-Royal train station, which killed 4 and wounded 170. These attacks represented a spillover from Algeria where the national government, supported by France, resisted the rise of Islamist political movements. After

3 consular agents were kidnapped in Algiers on October 24, 1993, and fearing an imminent spread of Islamist violence into France itself, authorities launched a crackdown across France, taking 110 people into custody over the course of two days in November. French interests have also been targeted after 9/11, as the Marsaud Report, a 2005 account of French counterterrorism efforts carried out by a parliamentary commission, made clear: "The absence of Islamist attacks on French soil since 9/11 should not be misinterpreted: it does not signify at all that France has been immunized from such actions, notably because of its position on the Iraq conflict. Elsewhere, we have already indicated that terrorist cells have been taken apart [since 9/11]—cells which were planning attacks on our soil. Further, outside of our national territory, French targets were struck, like the May 8, 2002, attack in Karachi . . . or the attack against the oil tanker *Limburg* off of Yemen on October 6, 2002. France is an integral part of Western civilization, a target of radical Islamic terrorists. In this regard, she figures among the potential targets of these terrorists to the same extent as any other Western nation."

In other words, France has not at all avoided being targeted, and it has not escaped major attacks through concessions or appeasement (as with the Spanish response to the Madrid bombing and the subsequent withdrawal of troops from Iraq). Rather it has been the specific French success of a counterterrorism strategy that has matured over more than two decades. French intelligence services were largely helpless in the face of the 1980 attacks carried out by Middle East terrorist organizations, and in the following two decades France was often regarded as a terrorist haven. Nonetheless, by the late 1990s, the French counterterrorism capacity had grown significantly, and was able to foil plots to launch attacks at the World Cup in 1998, the Strasbourg Cathedral in 2000, and the American Embassy in 2001.

The crux of the French counterterrorism strategy, based on 1986 legislation, centralizes all judicial procedures concerning terrorism in the Trial Court of Paris, where a cadre of judges could develop a specialized expertise. If a local prosecutor encounters evidence that a crime may be related to terrorism, it is referred to Paris immediately. The prosecution of terrorists is not stymied by limited resources in provincial offices, since all cases go to Paris, and there they can benefit from the concentration of attention and experience. These magistrates, or *juges d'instruction,* are charged with conducting impartial investigations and vested with considerable authority to conduct inquiries, authorize searches, permit wiretaps, and other matters which, in the United States, would require independent judicial oversight. Given their specialization in terrorism cases, they represent a potent force, particularly due to close collaboration with the domestic security service, the *Direction de la Surveillance du Territoire* (DST), which reports to the minister of the interior. This de facto cooperation between judiciary and executive powers, evidently foreign to American expectations of a separation of powers, accounts for much of the effectiveness of counterterrorism operations in France. It is also symptomatic of an openness within the French political system to a centralization of power, which might elsewhere be viewed as a threat to civil liberties.

Considerable civil and human rights objections have been raised, particularly with regard to the authority of the investigating magistrates to order preventive roundups and to authorize detentions. In 1995 a wave of arrests led to the detention of 131 individuals; another roundup in 1998 detained

53. Critics have denounced these mass arrests as "media spec-
tacles," or they have used the French term *rafle,* which carries
with it the memory of Nazi-era attacks on French Jews. In
addition, critics have complained that new laws criminalizing
conspiracies, rather than terrorist actions themselves, allow for
the further deployment of police power as a preventive mea-
sure. This shift to crime prevention is seen as a threatening
expansion of state power. Yet the magistrates have pointed
out that only through prevention strategies have attacks like
that planned for the World Cup at the Stade de France been
thwarted.

More recently, French counterterrorism practices have become the target of international criticism on the part of human
rights NGOs. Of particular concern is the prosecutorial use of
the charge "criminal association in relation to a terrorist undertaking," which is, in effect, a conspiracy charge. Membership in terrorist organizations is criminalized in France and in
many European countries, in contrast to the United States,
where the mere fact of membership is not sanctioned. France
faced extensive criticism in reports by Human Rights Watch
in 2007 and 2008 and again in a 2008 review by the UN
Human Rights Committee. Amnesty International raised similar charges against France in its 2009 report. According to
Human Rights Watch, French counterterrorism practices are
incompatible with the right of suspects to a fair trial. Specific
objections include the fact that suspects, once arrested, may
have to wait four to six days before seeing a judge or being
released; they may see a lawyer only after three or four days,
and then only for thirty minutes; suspects may be subjected
to questioning without the presence of a lawyer; and police
are not obligated to inform suspects that they may remain
silent. The primary target of criticism is, however, the pre-

emptive approach to prosecute a "criminal association in relation to a terrorist undertaking," which was established as a separate offense in 1996. According to Human Rights Watch, "this charge allows the authorities to intervene with the aim of preventing terrorism well before the commission of a crime. No specific terrorist act need be planned, much less executed, to give rise to the offense. Intended to criminalize all preparatory acts short of direct complicity in a terrorist plot, an *association de malfaiteurs* charge may be leveled for providing any kind of logistical or financial support to, or associating in a sustained fashion with, groups allegedly formed with the ultimate goal of engaging in terrorist activity."

For Human Rights Watch, this broad definition that enables preventive counterterrorism practices undermines fundamental rights. "The broad definition and expansive interpretation of *association de malfaiteurs* translate into a low standard of proof for decisions to arrest suspects or to place them under investigation by a judge. Indeed, casting a wide net to ensnare large numbers of people who might have some connection with an alleged terrorist network has been one of the characteristics of investigations into *association de malfaiteurs*." In addition, Amnesty International has pilloried the 2008 legislation authorizing preventive detention: after completing a sentence, an individual who is deemed dangerous may face an extension of sentencing for renewable one-year periods. Moreover, the police were empowered to develop files on any individual older than thirteen who represents a potential threat to public order.

These are powerful civil-libertarian objections to the centralization and expansion of policing powers in France. Nonetheless, the critics have been forced to recognize that all these

measures have taken place on the basis of French legislation—
that is, within the scope of the rule of law—without any
resorting to extrajudicial institutions, such as Guantánamo.
Moreover, they build on a tradition of the powerful republican
state that has deep roots in French political culture. Just as
modern political terror has its origins in the French Revolution, so too does the elaborate counterterrorist security appa-
ratus. Yet the strongest rebuttal to the critics remains success:
once the current system of counterterrorism institutions was
put in place in the mid-1990s, France has had much greater
success in preventing Islamist terrorist attacks—despite its
large immigrant population—than have other European
countries.

Culture Wars

The French response to Islamist terrorism extends beyond the
specific strategies of counterterrorism and the French role in
international politics and military strategy. To gain a full understanding of France facing jihad, it is indispensable to pay
attention to multiple cultural dimensions as well. Of course,
culture plays a role everywhere, but its significance is particularly important in France for several reasons: it is the home
of the largest Muslim community in Europe (just as it houses
the largest Jewish community, which adds to the complexity
of the situation). The size of the immigrant population in-
creases the importance of examining questions of immigrant
integration, which are ultimately cultural questions, rather
than focusing solely on the core networks of jihadist activists.
Moreover, while the issue is Islamism—a radical ideology that
depends on a particular interpretation of Islam—rather than
Islam in general, to claim that religion plays no role would

have little credibility. Yet matters of religion are particularly contentious in France given its emphatic culture of secularism. That hostility to religion derives from the French Enlightenment and is a core tenet of the republican legacy. Finally, culture is necessarily a prominent component of an analysis of the French response to terrorism precisely because of the prominence of intellectual life in France with its long history of applauding political violence and, since Jean-Jacques Rousseau in the eighteenth century, an animus against civilization, often coupled with a celebration of primitivism.

In France, more than elsewhere, concern with terrorism has taken the shape of an anxiety with the emergence of immigrant communities resistant to integration into mainstream culture. In other countries, notions of multiculturalism welcomed the development of distinct ethnic and religious subcultures; in France, a fundamental expectation of entry into the shared community of the French republic has prevailed. If the French Revolution's ideal of equality always implied an imperative for homogenization—getting rid of differences— this took on a particular saliency in the first decade of the twenty-first century. As the conflict between the West and Islamism grew sharper, fears of a domestic radicalism and homegrown terror began to grow. At the same time, certain outward signs indicated a greater turn toward Islam within the immigrant community. In other words, despite the standard sociological expectation of gradual secularization and the disappearance of religion, a contrary perception of some greater Islamic identification began to take hold.

The flashpoint for conflict became the wearing of the hijab, or headscarf, by Muslim women. For some this represented a worrisome return to religion and a rejection of secular modernity; others argued that women were subject to patriarchal pressure and forced by their families to submit to the headscarf; still others defended the headscarf as an indication of a woman's free choice to declare her religion. Whatever the causal explanation, the headscarf was taken as a declaration of religious identity and, as such, it was targeted by 2004 legislation during Chirac's presidency: wearing the hijab was banned in all public schools, along with any other ostentatious displays of religion, such as large crucifixes or the Jewish *keepa*. Although the government framed the legislation in a way to appear to treat all religions equally, the character of the debate made clear that the genuine target was Islamic symbolism, even if Christian and Jewish accessories had to be sacrificed as well.

Mass demonstrations took place against the law in France and abroad, but in the end it was adopted, with a very high rate of support among the French electorate. Since then the controversy has subsided and the law has been upheld in the European Court of Human Rights. (While the headscarf is banned in French schools, it can be worn in French universities; in contrast, in Turkey the headscarf is banned in universities.) Ultimately, French secularist traditions stand at odds with the dramatic demonstrations of religious membership: in 2009 the matter reemerged in a discussion to ban the full-length cloaks of Muslim women, the burqa and the niqab (the latter leaves the eyes uncovered). The clothing is seen not only as a marker of identity but also as an indication of the subordination of women within Islam. Its critics therefore argue that an egalitarian society should banish blatant markers of inequality. In fact, the prohibition on the headscarf in school and the proposed legislation against the niqab should be seen against the backdrop of wider feminist critiques of Islam and practices within immigrant communities. In this context, the group *Ni Putes Ni Soumises* (Neither Whores Nor Submissives), founded by French Muslim women in 2002 in response to violence against women in the *banlieues,* has highlighted issues of gender conflict within the French Muslim world.

France houses large Muslim and Jewish communities— including many Jewish immigrants from North Africa. Given the tensions in the Middle East, the intense focus in much of the Muslim world on the plight of the Palestinians, and the radicalization of parts of the immigrant Muslim community during the past decade, anti-Jewish sentiment has been on the rise. While anti-Semitism traditionally was reserved primarily, if not exclusively, to the French right, it has now migrated to the immigrant community and to parts of the left. Synagogues and other Jewish institutions have been attacked, and an anti-Semitic discourse has made its way into French popular culture. To be sure, not all Arab anti-Semitism is jihadist, but the jihadist ideology of Islamist terrorism is endemically anti-Semitic, radicalizing and amplifying some traditionalist Muslim images in order to justify the holy war against "Jews and Crusaders."

Two particular events of the past decade stand out as indicators of this new French anti-Semitism. The first, a complicated media event, involves an alleged shooting in Gaza in September 2000 during the intifada. Charles Enderlin, a journalist for France 2 television, reported that a Palestinian boy, Muhammed al-Durrah, was killed by shots from the Israeli position at Netzarim Junction. While the Israel Defense Forces initially apologized for the shooting, many doubts were subsequently raised about the incident. Suggestions have been made that the shots may have come from Palestinian fighters or even that the boy was never really hit. Enderlin, who in fact had not been present but relied solely on the reports of his cameraman, faced accusations of mounting a hoax, which in turn led to litigation. His adversary, French media critic Philippe Karsenty, was vindicated in the Paris Court of Appeal in 2009, but the matter has been appealed to a higher level and is, as of this writing, pending before the *Cour de Cassation*. At stake is the question of whether the French media establishment, which rallied to Enderlin's defense, has disseminated a false account that has contributed to the spread of a blood libel throughout the Muslim world. Indeed al-Durrah has become an iconic figure—his image appears on postage stamps, and streets have been named after him. He has also entered into the iconography of Islamist terrorism: Osama bin Laden made reference to him in a public statement, and his image appears in the background of the filmed beheading of American journalist Daniel Pearl. In this complex affair, French media politics and the Middle East conflict overlap with the brutal imagery of jihadism. Terrorism is not only the conspiracy and the violence but the whole cycle of representation and recrimination that provides pretexts for further killings.

The second event sheds light on the proximity of anti-Semitic Muslim violence and the criminal milieu of the *banlieues*. On January 21, 2006, Ilan Halimi, a twenty-three-year-old French Jew, was kidnapped by a gang made up largely of Muslim members, including some juveniles, and which called itself revealingly the "gang of barbarians." Held captive for more than three weeks in a housing project in Bagneux, just south of Paris, Halimi was tortured extensively, while the gang attempted to extort ransom from his family. Gang members lately explained that because they knew Halimi was Jewish, they assumed he was wealthy; in fact, Halimi came from a modest background and lived in the same neighborhood as his captors. He was eventually abandoned outdoors in the winter weather; although rushed to a hospital, he succumbed to his multiple wounds and the strains of exposure. The trial took place in 2009 and attracted extensive public attention; the ringleader, Youssouf Fofana, received a life sentence while other defendants were treated less severely, depending on their degrees of involvement.

For our purposes the key question is the relationship between this violence and Islamist terrorism. While the "barbarians" may not have been principally political and there is no evidence of religious fervor, police reportedly found radical fundamentalist literature during one arrest. To what extent does such evidence demonstrate an explicit ideological motivation? Members of the group were also involved in other extortion attempts and drug trafficking. Within this social milieu, popularized anti-Semitism combined with criminal behavior and sporadically radical Islamist identifications. It is surely not the case that the Halimi murder can be equated fully with jihadist terror, but it highlights the context in which terrorism incubates. It also provides an allegory of the proximity of terrorist violence and venal criminality: the point is not to excuse terrorism as merely criminal, but to recognize how, at the level of everyday life in the violent slums of the French *banlieues,* political ideologies and religious stereotypes provide opportunities to mask a criminal agenda. Whatever "ideals" they may expound, one should not lose sight of how much straightforward crime—such as the drug trade— motivates the Taliban, Al Qaeda, and their supporters around the world. Meanwhile, the Halimi killing remains a chilling indication of the potential for anti-Semitic violence in the heart of France: a kind of everyday terrorism.

Yet one can hardly be surprised by politicized violence in light of French history. The philosopher Jean-Paul Sartre's notorious endorsement of anticolonial killing in his introduction to Frantz Fanon's *Wretched of the Earth* provided a classic justification of violence in the name of third-world liberation. It was the same Sartre who later lent his prestige to the Baader-Meinhof terrorists in West Germany, whose links both to Palestinian radicals and the Communist East German intelligence network have come to light in recent years. French left intellectuals have a long history of cultivating an adulation and admiration for violent extremists in their various wars on Western modernity. In the same vein, the historian and cultural theoretician Michel Foucault celebrated the violence of Ayatollah Khomeini's Iranian Revolution in 1979. There seems to be an anti-civilizational instinct hardwired into French intellectual life that draws on Rousseau's eighteenth-century celebration of nature against the presumed corruption of the city and the court. More than two hundred years later, the French sociologist Jean Baudrillard expressed his understanding and sympathy for the terrorists of 9/11, taken to represent an authenticity of life against what Baudrillard deemed the banality of American existence.

With that bias in the intellectual tradition, it is noteworthy that a generation of French intellectuals, writers, and philosophers has emerged that has begun to articulate a critique of terrorism, Islamism, and the multicultural predispositions that tend to provide apologies for Islamist violence. The novelist Michel Houellebecq has dissected Islamist antipathy to the West as well as the reluctance of the West to offer a robust response, especially in his novel *Platform* as well as in interviews. The philosopher Alain Finkielkraut has analyzed the politics around Islamist violence, especially the civil unrest in

France. While much of the liberal media tended to apologize for the riots as expressions of socioeconomic problems and to blame the government for insufficient social services, Finkielkraut bluntly described them as "anti-republic pogroms" and complained that political correctness prevented commentators from expressing critical judgments on violence by immigrants. Comparing the riots in French cities to a notorious anti-immigrant mob in the former East Germany, he commented, "Imagine for a moment that they were whites, like in Rostock in Germany. Right away, everyone would have said: 'Fascism won't be tolerated.' When an Arab torches a school, it's rebellion. When a white guy does it, it's fascism. I'm 'color blind.' Evil is evil, no matter what color it is." He claimed to be "color blind," but in politically correct France, he faced accusations of racism for precisely this comment.

Yet the most notorious case of the French intellectual response to Islamist terrorism involves a philosopher and high school teacher, Robert Redeker. In an essay published in the conservative daily *Le Figaro* in September 2006, Redeker elaborated on the reactions to the address that Pope Benedict XVI had recently delivered in Regensburg, Germany. Benedict had raised questions about the relationship of Islam to violence: the result was violent uprisings in much of the Muslim world. Redeker's essay—"What Should the Free World Do in the Face of Islamist Intimidation?"—zeroed in on the representations of violence and conquest in the Koran itself: the question of holy war, Mohammed's treatment of his adversaries, and the centrality of violence to the doctrine.

The point of the essay was to call upon the West not to knuckle under to the threats of Islamist terror. "As in the Cold War, where violence and intimidation were the methods used by an ideology hell-bent on hegemony, so today Islam tries to put its leaden mantle all over the world. Benedict XVI's cruel experience is testimony to this. Nowadays, the West has to be called the 'free world' in comparison to the Muslim world; likewise, the enemies of the 'free world,' the zealous bureaucrats of the Koran's vision, swarm in the very center of the free World." The response to the essay was immediate and brutal. Quickly translated into Arabic, it was denounced on Al Jazeera. *Le Figaro* backed down, apologized for the publication, and removed the essay from its website. Meanwhile, Redeker faced an onslaught of death threats, and his name, photograph, and home address were posted on jihadist websites. He and his family were forced into hiding. The journalist Caroline Fourest compared the affair to the fatwa issued by Khomeini against the Anglo-Indian author Salman Rushdie for his novel *The Satanic Verses.* While important members of the French intellectual life rallied around Redeker and the right of free expression, many public figures only offered lukewarm responses or even chose to condemn Redeker. If his criticism had been directed against Christianity, there is no doubt that he would have received nearly universal support, but because he was critical of Islam, French intellectual life was prepared to see him sacrificed, along with the principle of free speech.

In the end, France remains internally divided. It has been able to conduct admirably successful counterterrorism strategies and, when all is said and done, it remains engaged in Afghanistan in the war against Islamist terror. Facing the challenges of immigration, especially from Muslim countries, it envisions an integrationist strategy of immigration, despite the many signs of its failing. At the same time, its national ambitions have meant carving out an alternative strategy to the United States: for Chirac, that involved playing the anti-Amer-

ican card during the Iraq war—but for Sarkozy there are in-
dications that it means critiquing the accommodationist tendencies in the Obama administration's response to the Iranian
efforts to develop nuclear weapons. In comments at the United
Nations in September 2009, the French president distanced
himself from the American "dream" of disarmament, commenting, "President Obama himself has said that he dreams
of a world without nuclear weapons. Before our very eyes,
two countries are doing exactly the opposite at this very moment. Since 2005, Iran has violated five Security Council Res-
olutions. . . . I support America's 'extended hand.' But what
have these proposals for dialogue produced for the international community? Nothing but more enriched uranium and
more centrifuges. And, last but not least, it has resulted in a
statement by Iranian leaders calling for wiping off the map a
member of the United Nations. What are we to do? What
conclusions are we to draw? At a certain moment hard facts
will force us to make decisions."

The question of Islamist terrorism is a broad one: it involves primarily terrorist organizations, like Al Qaeda, but
they exist in a field of violence that stretches from the *ban-
lieue* delinquency of the "Gang of Barbarians" to the barbarian
regime in Tehran and its aspirations for nuclear firepower.
France has responded variously to these complex challenges:
if its leadership against the war of Iraq, its sympathy for Saddam Hussein, its corruption through the oil-for-food scandal,
and its intellectuals' solidarity with terrorists have been sad-
dening, one should not, alternatively, overlook the other side
of France: the success of French counterterrorism, the aspirations for integration, the critique of multiculturalism, and
the strident voices of writers like Houllebecq, Fourest, Finkielkraut, and Redeker.

.

CHAPTER FOUR

Germany

Memory and Modernization

For no country in Europe does the past weigh as heavily on the present as it does for Germany. The scars of two world wars and two dictatorships—Nazism and East German Communism—are deep and continue to define political debates and national identity in complex and sometimes unpredictable ways. The historical memory of Prussian militarism is typically taken to be a cautionary tale against military adventures, regardless as to whether the military—as opposed to other elements of German society and politics—deserves to bear all the blame that is attributed to it. That problem of historical interpretation aside, the ravages of the First and Second World Wars, both the suffering caused by Germans and the suffering Germans experienced, indisputably represent a legacy that makes Germans today very apprehensive about participation in military engagements. The 1955 decision for the Federal Republic (West Germany) to join NATO, as a bulwark against the Soviet threat, was controversial; so was German participation in the Balkans war of the 1990s; and the German role in Afghanistan today remains a flashpoint of political debate. Yet West Germany did join NATO, and unified Germany participated in the Balkans, just as German soldiers play an important, if strictly limited, role in Afghanistan in the fight against Islamist terrorism.

The NATO-led International Security Assistance Force (ISAF) in Afghanistan numbered 67,700 troops as of July 2009 (in addition to the 90,000 troops of the Afghan National Army and 80,000 Afghan police). Among the national contingents, the Germans (4,245) number third, well behind the United States and the United Kingdom, but considerably ahead of France (3,070), Canada (2,830), or Italy (2,795). In this front of the war on Islamist terrorism, the German presence is not inconsiderable. The German forces are located in the north of the country, providing assistance to the national government in maintaining security and reconstruction. However, the Bundestag, expressing the German apprehension regarding military engagement, generally restricts the Bundeswehr from participating in combat against the Taliban in the south or east. Still, the German contingent has undertaken combat in the north, killing at least 107 Taliban and arresting others. As of May 2009, 32 German soldiers and 3 policemen had been killed, 18 of them by enemy fire, and 117 German troops and police had been wounded. While the U.S. government has hoped to encourage greater German presence in Afghanistan, the scope of German participation is already significantly greater than that of any other European country except England. Germany might be able to afford to do more—although an increase would be politically controversial—but plenty of European allies are doing less.

In fact, the current level of German participation in ISAF comes regularly under attack within Germany from political opponents, just as it faces doubts in the press—not unlike the criticism that the U.S. presence in Afghanistan also faces from domestic opponents in politics and the public sphere. Similar debates rage in Britain. The German ambivalence about the Afghan front in the war on terror is then hardly distinctly German but, being German, it is more starkly ambivalent. "Two souls dwell, alas, within my breast," spoke Goethe's Faust, and that could well be a motto for the German response to Islamist terrorism: to fight or not to fight.

While the memory of wars past encourages a pacifist predisposition skeptical of any foreign military deployment, memory also casts a shadow on domestic counterterrorism issues. Some Germans can recall the Nazi rise to power and draw the plausible conclusion that a muscular state ought to squelch lawlessness and maintain the rule of law as the precondition for a functioning democracy. The state should exercise, as Max Weber famously declared, a monopoly on violence; therefore, the violence of any paramilitary forces should be disallowed. The Weimar state's failure to stop Nazi and Communist violence paved the way to its own demise. The lesson some draw from that sorry past is that a democratic state should mount a strong defense of the rule of law and not allow violent lawlessness to fester: just as West German democracy responded harshly and vigorously to the challenge of the Baader-Meinhof terrorism of the 1970s, so has it pursued a forceful counterterrorism agenda in the face of the Islamist threat, under the leadership of both the center-left Social Democratic interior minister Otto Schily and the center-right Christian Democratic interior minister Wolfgang Schäuble.

However, such forceful policing measures also provoke civil libertarian anxieties about the growth of a repressive state. Here too the German past casts a long shadow: memories of the Gestapo or the East German Stasi generate a heightened sensitivity to any expansion of police powers or surveillance practices. Again, this dynamic is not thoroughly different from debates in the United States and the objections to measures like the Patriot Act, viewed by some as an unwarranted expansion of state power. Yet in Germany, such anxieties about surveillance, control, and curtailments of rights have a greater resonance in light of the experience of two police states. "Law and order" can have as negative a ring in Germany as in the United States, if not more so. One of the features of the German political landscape that would seem counterintuitive to many American observers is that the shift to the right brought about by the election of October 2009, which replaced the "grand coalition" of Social Democrats and Conservatives with the center-right coalition of Conservatives with the small, "liberal" Free Democratic Party (FDP)—which is classically liberal, combining a free-market agenda with civil liberties concerns—may translate into some limits on intrusive counterterrorism measures and greater awareness of civil liberties. At least the program of the new government suggests that classical liberalism may be a better guardian of rights than is the tradition of welfare-state social democracy.

It is, however, in the nature of the contemporary confrontation with Islamist terrorism that it is played out on multiple fronts with blurred borders and multiple overlaps. It is a complex narrative with multiple components. One story involves bona fide military engagement, especially in Afghanistan: defending German national security in the Hindu Kush, as the former Social Democratic minister of defense, Peter Struck, put it. Another story involves the efforts to ferret out terrorist networks and sleeper cells before they strike—sooner or later, some fear, what happened in Madrid in 2004 and in London in 2005 will take place in Germany. Yet another story concerns the way German society, culture, and political institutions have interacted with the growing Muslim population, which began to increase in the 1950s as low-wage laborers came from Turkey (and many Southern European countries) to work in the German *Wirtschaftswunder,* the rapid postwar rebuilding, but now includes significant numbers of Iranians and Arabs as well. Germany has had a difficult time integrating these foreigners: obtaining citizenship remains difficult (even for the members of these communities born in Germany) and ghetto-like enclaves have expanded in many German cities.

Especially in the wave of German national sentiment after unification in 1991, signs of xenophobia, or *Ausländerfeindlichkeit,* became ominously apparent, including mob violence against immigrants and refugees. Those political currents fed some resurgence of an anti-immigrant and sometimes neo-Nazi far right that has gained ground in certain areas on the local and regional level, but, so far, not in national politics. (When all is said and done, the xenophobic far right is much less prominent in Germany than in France or Italy, let alone parts of Central Europe, although it is again German history that magnifies the concern about the emergence of racist politics there.) The broad center of German politics rejects the far-right agenda, although concerns abound about the integration of new immigrants into the modern, secular, and liberal values of contemporary German society. Muslim immigrants, often from rural and traditionalist areas of Turkey, bring with them habits of socialization that end up at odds with the expectations of modern Germany. Many hope that immigrants will come to accept those values of modernity and participate in German culture, the hegemonic set of ideals that define the Federal Republic of Germany.

The German-Syrian scholar Bassam Tibi named these values the *Leitkultur,* the primary culture, which immigrants ought to adopt. As is often the case, it is a democratically progressive and pro-Western Muslim who advocates integration and criticizes immigrants who try to re-create traditionalist (or pseudo-traditionalist) lifestyles in the midst of the modern metropolis. Ironically—or sadly—it is also often the case that otherwise progressive and even leftist Germans argue for multiculturalism, with the implication that backward habits, in gender relations, for example, brought with immigrants to Germany are deemed to deserve unconditional respect as an alternative way of life, which, thanks to a bashful cultural relativism, cannot be subject to criticism. The particularly dramatic flashpoint for this conflict involves the question of "honor killings"—Muslim women who choose a modern lifestyle have been murdered by male family members in order to preserve family "honor." In some court cases, "cultural defenses" have been accepted—that is, specific cultural traditions have been treated as mitigating circumstances for crimes. The critique of such relativism has added to the calls for the need for a *Leitkultur.* In addition, because members of immigrant communities frequently have lower levels of education, suffer from the challenges of a foreign country, and are caught in the particular trap of a welfare-state economy— relatively high unemployment and state subsidies that discourage beneficiaries from joining the workforce—high crime levels, especially violent juvenile delinquency, have begun to develop. This in turn only feeds public worries about immigration, integration, and Islam.

As has been underscored previously, however, Islam is not Islamism, and it would be foolish in addition to incorrect to misidentify the whole Muslim community in Germany as tinged with terrorism. Nor is the juvenile delinquency of Turkish youth in Kreuzberg or Neukölln, areas of high immigrant concentration in the center of Berlin, the same as terrorist plots. Confusing these distinct issues is not only erroneous—it could also end up pushing large sectors of the Muslim immigrant communities, the moderate or unpolitical spectrum of opinion, into the welcoming arms of Islamist recruiters. However, it would also be foolish to ignore precisely that point of contact and recruitment; alienation and disaffection in the immigrant community can in certain instances burgeon into terror, as was the case with the London bombings. There have been enough near hits and foiled plots in Germany to have made the public alert to the possibility of homegrown terror. Moreover, the international jihadist networks facilitate the mobility of potential recruits from Germany or elsewhere in Europe (or the United States) to training camps in the Middle East. Islamism can fly under the flag of Islam, even when it manipulates and distorts it. This is why the military response to terrorism, as exemplified by the German soldiers stationed in Afghanistan, cannot be fully separated from the efforts to thwart terrorist plots in Germany, and this transnational connection in turn is, ultimately, not sealed off hermetically from the social problems and cultural disaffection that mar the immigrant experience. This overlap notwithstanding, one should not ignore the very many Muslim immigrants to Germany eager to embrace Western lifestyles and values—from outspoken intellectuals to young women trying to escape arranged marriages—who often bear the brunt of ostracism or worse. They too are part of the German response to Islamist terror.

The Challenge of Domestic Terrorism

In September 2007, German security forces succeeded in breaking up an Islamist terror cell that had sought cover in the tiny village of Oberschlendorn in an idyllic tourist region, the Sauerland, of western Germany. The trial of the Sauerland group turned into the largest terrorism prosecution since the 1970s and the campaign against the RAF, or "Red Army Fraction," known as the Baader-Meinhof group. Three men were taken at the initial arrest, where 26 detonators and 12 drums of hydrogen peroxide were found, the same explosive used in attacks on the London transport system. A fourth member, who had fled, was apprehended near the Pakistani border. Two members were German converts to Islam, one was a German national of Turkish background, and the fourth a Turkish citizen. As of this writing, the main trial is still underway, but in October 2009, some collaborators were convicted for supporting a terrorist group, the Islamic Jihad Union. The outcome of the trial involved relatively limited procurement of material for the IJU in Pakistan, which the defendants had all visited. However, because they cooperated with the prosecution and offered confessions, the severity of the sentences was blunted. In fact, Sauerland group members participated in attacks on American troops in Afghanistan and planned attacks in Germany, especially on Americans, on the scale of the September 11 killings. "They wanted to see cities burn, like New York. People would die and sink into mourning to face their own guilt. The heathen West was supposed to get an unforgettable lesson, and the brothers in faith in Afghanistan, Pakistan, and Iraq were going to see just what German converts were able to do." In addition, and equally disturbing, they reported organizing recruitment efforts, sending new fighters from Germany to the battlefields of Pakistan and Afghanistan. Adem Yilmaz confessed to recruiting six young men, sending them from Germany to Pakistan, including one who died on March 3, 2008, in a suicide attack on an ISAF camp in Afghanistan, killing four soldiers.

The Sauerland trial is, however, hardly Germany's first encounter with Islamist terrorism. On July 31, 2006, Jihad Hamad and Youssef el-Hajdib placed suitcase bombs in two local trains. Although they failed to detonate due to faulty construction, the suitcase bomb affair made it clear that Germany was not immune to the spread of Islamist terror. Public concern with issues of domestic security began to grow, and the Sauerland plot, given the scope of the intended violence, has brought the terrorist threat to the forefront of public attention.

Yet even before 9/11, violence from the Muslim world had spilled over into Germany. On April 5, 1986, the LaBelle discotheque in West Berlin, a favored venue of U.S. servicemen, was attacked. Plastic explosives that had been placed under the DJ booth detonated, leaving 3 dead and 230 wounded, including 50 U.S. soldiers. In the wake of the attack, U.S. intelligence intercepted telex messages of congratulations from Libya to the Libyan embassy in East Berlin. It was not until 2001, however, that a Libyan diplomat, two Palestinians, and the German wife of one of them were convicted for the bombing. Middle East politics had shed blood in Berlin.

The LaBelle bombing belongs, however, to another context; it was a chapter in the history of U.S. tensions with Libya framed by the Cold War. Similarly, the even earlier intersection between Baader-Meinhof and Palestinian terrorism was rooted in another era—the New Left's turn to violence and its exoticist fascination with third-world revolution—even if that particular collaboration between German radicals and terrorist anti-Zionism presaged the unique attraction that Arab extremism would later hold for the German left. That specific nexus involves the magnetic pull Arab opposition to Israel can exercise on Germans burdened by their country's history of anti-Semitism. In a paradoxical psychology, violent anti-Zionism could provide post-Holocaust Germans with a therapeutic purging of their own Nazi legacy. By identifying the Jewish state as a perpetrator of crimes, German extremists could unburden themselves of any sense of national guilt for the crimes and genocide carried out by the Nazis.

Yet the collaboration between the RAF and Palestinian radicals, like the Libyan bombing in Berlin, took place long ago, at a historical moment defined by the ideological and cultural anxieties of a divided Europe, before the fall of Communism. It was only once the divided world of the Cold War came to an end—and nowhere more dramatically than in Berlin and in Germany—that the seeds of Islamism, germinating for decades, genuinely began to sprout in Europe. Once the Soviets, who had invaded Afghanistan and faced a popular and Islam-driven insurgency there, were defeated internationally, Muslim radicals could begin to carry a radicalized Islam from the mujahadeen of Central Asia across the Middle East and the Balkans and into the heart of Europe. The violence of Islamist terrorism depends on the virulence of an extremist religious loyalty that has in many profound ways taken the place of the leftist and Communist ideologies of the 1970s and 1980s: Islamism is the new Communism, at least in the sense of an ideology that provides a justification to extremists to carry out acts of violence against the institutions of free and democratic societies. The difference between LaBelle—a case of state-sponsored terrorism in the context of the Cold War—and the Sauerland group, an independent cell with ties to Al Qaeda, indicates a dramatic generational change in the character of terror: but both cases involve a stark confrontation between free societies and their terrorist enemies.

State Responses: Prevention and Prosecution

The primary responsibility for security, counterterrorism, and crime prevention in Germany lies with the interior minister (comparable to the U.S. attorney general), an office occupied since 9/11 by two distinctive political figures who have opted for robust responses to the threat of Islamist terror and therefore became lightning rods for political controversy and personal vilification. A look at these two key personalities, their conceptual visions, and their policy initiatives provides some textured insight into the politics and possibilities of the German response to terrorism.

Certainly one of the most intriguing figures in the broad story of the European reaction to terror is Otto Schily. Born in 1932, he studied law and opened his practice in 1963. Drawing close to the radical student movement of the 1960s—he was a friend of the German student leader Rudi Dutschke—he gained widespread notoriety in the 1970s as the forceful and adept defender of terrorists in and around the Baader-Meinhof gang: Gudrun Ensslin and Horst Mahler. A founding member of the left-wing ecological Green Party in 1980, Schily was elected to the Bundestag in 1983; in 1989 he switched party affiliation to the Social Democrats and was then reelected to the Bundestag; in 1998 he was appointed interior minister, serving until 2005, under Chancellor Gerhard Schröder.

As ironic as it may seem that a former terrorist lawyer would become the head of German law enforcement, the astonishing twist in the story is that Schily was not only responsible for German law enforcement but in fact became an outspoken advocate of tougher law-and-order policies. For example, he vigorously advocated for the inclusion of biometric data (fingerprints) in passports to provide heightened security controls, a policy that began to be implemented in 2005. In the wake of the attacks in New York and Washington, Schily pushed for significantly tighter regulations to protect Germany from terrorists. These included expanded cooperation with intelligence services in other countries and much more elaborate monitoring of foreign individuals seeking entry into Germany, including the many international students hoping to attend German universities. Such monitoring would depend however on extensive data collection: counterterrorism began to generate policies of elaborate surveillance.

In an interview with *Der Spiegel,* Schily asserted that "we have to ensure that people are not smuggled into the country or sneak in on their own under false pretenses, whether they claim economic or humanitarian grounds, if they have some other motive altogether. To do this, we need all the data available to our security forces. And we need the visa data from (foreign) embassies to be available to our police and security forces." Yet not all politicians were as adamant about an expansion of police surveillance powers, particularly against the background of German history. Johannes Rau, then president of Germany, declared that "A totally protected everyday life is no longer free." Confronted with that fear of a potential police state, Schily replied that "No one wants to stand guard over every step and every movement people take. That's a red herring." In other words, he dismissed his opponents' nightmare vision of a panoptical state, omniscient and omnipresent, as a propagandistic exaggeration. On the contrary, he continued, "Whoever wants to live in freedom needs to be safe from crime and terrorism. That is what people are really concerned with, and not with dusty theories about some allegedly inescapable Surveillance State. That's why a recent poll shows that only 17 percent of Germans are skeptical about the counterterrorism measures; and nearly 80 percent support my policies." The Social Democratic interior minister could point to a German electorate clamoring for security, despite left-liberal apprehensions about invasions of privacy and the expansion of police powers.

This aggressive pursuit of expanded intelligence sources led Schily to a further step, which only became public in 2007, two years after he had left office. At stake is the expansion of the war on terror into the brave new cybernetic world. In 2005, Schily approved an enlargement of the scope of online monitoring permissible to government security forces. This enhanced monitoring not only involved tracking websites and chat rooms but also opened the door for intelligence services to use Internet connections to gain access to end-user hard drives. To many, this elaboration of intelligence gathering appeared to be an unreasonable infringement of personal privacy. The president of the Federal Constitutional Court, Hans-Jürgen Papier, warned publicly that the state must be cautious about going too far in the pursuit of security, and the head of data protection declared that the state not only has an obligation to provide security but also to guarantee civil liberties. Despite such hesitations indicative of the vibrant civil-liberties culture that has developed in Germany—surely more than anywhere else on the European continent—the Social-Democratic interior minister adamantly ratcheted up security technologies in the face of the Islamist threat.

Schily's successor as interior minister, the conservative Wolfgang Schäuble, could not have been different: where Schily emerged from the New Left, Schäuble has deep roots in the Christian Democratic Party, as a member of which he has served in the Bundestag since 1972. He served as interior minister from 1989 to 1991 under Helmut Kohl and, in that capacity, he led the West German negotiations with East Germany over the terms of the treaty of unification. He returned to the Interior Ministry nearly fifteen years later, after Schily left in 2005. In 1990 a mentally deranged would-be assassin shot him in the wake of a campaign event, leaving him paralyzed and in a wheel chair. In the wake of the 2009 elections and the change in the ruling coalition in Berlin, Schäuble moved from the Interior Ministry to become the minister of finance.

Schäuble continued Schily's tough policies and amplified them, all the while defending these steps toward greater security with an aggressive public presence. He vociferously defended the war in Iraq, despite its unpopularity in Germany; he has advocated for further online searches of private computers; he has proposed that biometric data (fingerprints) collected for passports be made digitally available for police investigations; and he has supported permitting the government to use the army, the Bundeswehr, in domestic operations. Even more controversially, he has called for a modification of the presumption of innocence in cases of terrorism: "The presumption of innocence basically means that we would rather not punish ten guilty people than punish one innocent. This principle cannot pertain when it involves preventing a danger. Would it be right to say: we would rather allow ten attacks to take place than try to stop someone who may have planned nothing at all? In my opinion, that would be wrong." In other words, the presumption of innocence pertains to individuals accused of having committed crimes; but in a preventive context, where a crime, or a terrorist attack, is anticipated, Schäuble argues that a similar protection of the individual rights of the accused is no longer rational. Perhaps his most controversial claim, however, involved the proposal in early 2007 to allow for shooting down hijacked passenger planes in order to prevent a 9/11 scenario in Germany.

For his opponents, such public and provocative speculation only added to the concern that the advocates of a war on terror were pushing up against and beyond the limits of the constitutional state. During the heated 2009 election, Schäuble's advocacy for expanded policing and counterterrorism measures was attacked not only from the left but also from the Free Democrats, the centrist and free-market liberal party. Sabine Leutheusser-Schnarrenberger, a leading FDP spokesperson on civil liberties, described Schäuble's agenda as "a list of horrors." Perhaps more than any other European country, Germany has shown deep divisions in the pursuit of an appropriate balance between security and civil liberties.

While Schäuble has stood out as a vociferous advocate of a tough conservative set of security policies, he has also distinguished himself, perhaps unexpectedly, in a quite different but ultimately related area of social policy: the integration of Muslim immigrants. Far from playing with far-right xenophobia or stoking fears about Islam, Schäuble, with his indisputable conservative credentials, has promoted integration and assimilation as integral to a successful counterterrorism strategy: in order to prevent Islamist terrorism, young Muslims have to be able to find productive pathways to success in German society. During the 1990s, when Germany made an effort to modernize its citizenship law to facilitate immigration, Schäuble strongly embraced the goal of integration and, therefore, also opposed the model of double citizenship, which he regarded as likely to impede an immigrant's genuine entry into German society and an internalization of its values. That policy position, the insistence that the immigrant enter into German culture and its contemporary values, stands at odds with the typically center-left multicultural agenda of sanctioning a diversity of values and therefore refraining from guiding immigrants into the German mainstream.

This cultural dimension and the disputes between integrationists and multiculturalists, clearly distinct from the debate over the array of policing measures, represents an additional front in Germany's encounter with Islam. As forcefully as Schäuble pursued counterterrorism initiatives against Islamist extremism, he has simultaneously endeavored to accelerate the assimilation of Muslim immigrants. In an address in Cairo, he underscored that Muslims have equal rights in Germany, and in Germany he has spoken of immigration as an enrichment of society. However, he has also warned against the concentration of immigrant populations in ghetto-like quarters—as is the case in the French *banlieues* and in some inner-city areas in Germany—and in 2006 he established an "Islam Conference" on the national level to serve as an interlocutor for the government with the Muslim community, parallel to similar structures for other religious groupings.

Muslims in Germany

The Interior Ministry, together with the Islam Conference, commissioned the first comprehensive survey of its kind, *Muslim Life in Germany,* which was released in June 2009. It found that there are 4.3 million Muslims in Germany (out of a general population of about 83 million—that is, some 5.18 percent), a million more than had been previously estimated. Nearly two-thirds have a Turkish background, reflecting the labor migration patterns of earlier decades, which was then followed by policies of family unification. The second largest group, 550,000 (or about 13 percent of Germany's Muslims), is Southeast European, largely refugees from the former Yugoslavia. Approximately 7.5 percent come from the Middle East. Less than half have German citizenship, reflecting the high hurdles to naturalization; only 2 percent live in the former East Germany, with its disproportionately high unemployment.

The study also demonstrates an unexpected degree of cultural integration, side by side with social disadvantage. More than half of Muslims in Germany older than 16 are members in a German organization or club, while only 4 percent belong exclusively to an association oriented to their country of origin (for example, a Turkish cultural association). To the extent that organization membership is an indicator of cultural orientation, many more immigrants are evidently involved with institutions that tie them to Germany than to their old country. Despite the prominence of religion in public debates, only 20 percent of German Muslims are associated with a religious community, presumably reflecting the strong tradition of secularism in Turkey (the primary source country) and the moderate religiosity in Bosnia (the second source country). Assuming a relatively low level of religious affiliation in the Muslim community, the Interior Ministry under Schäuble determined that the Islam Conference should not only include delegates of religious associations but also lay members—journalists, scholars, and professionals—as representatives of the general public. The study confirmed the legitimacy of this decision that Muslims in Germany should not be regarded solely as a religious grouping. On the contrary, they are members of diverse immigrant populations, potentially on their way toward assimilation and integration. In Germany—as elsewhere in Europe—Muslims are not a narrowly religious community, and certainly not a unified religious community, but are segmented into an array of disparate cultural and ethnic groupings.

This divergence between religion and cultural identification was further confirmed in surprising ways: While most German Muslims do want to see Islamic religious instruction take place in public schools (in Germany it is common for students to receive such instruction in their particular faith at school), few of them in fact observe religious practices on a regular basis. In the Turkish community, 70 percent report that they seldom or never attend religious ceremonies. Even among those women who describe themselves as very religious, only half report wearing a head covering in public. German Muslims may actually be becoming more like other Germans not only by virtue of their gradual move away from Islam but by their moving toward the same sort of post-religious secularism that characterizes much of mainstream Germany and Western Europe more broadly.

A further point of public controversy has involved sensationalist journalistic reports of special accommodations made for Muslim children in schools. However, the report found that only 7 percent of German Muslims wanted to have their daughters excused from swimming and only 4 percent preferred to keep their daughters out of sex education classes. That latter figure actually compares favorably with the 15 percent of all parents who object. Muslims appear to be more liberal than the overall population, at least on this point. While there is undoubtedly a small contingent of the Muslim community that resists mainstream culture, the vast majority may be moving toward integration. A greater hindrance to this integration, however, is not a matter of culture but of economic opportunity, strictly limited as a result of the low educational levels for the immigrant generation. Many of the original immigration generations arrived in Germany with minimal schooling. Their children are, however, typically more successful in German schools. In the spirit of the integration policy, Schäuble underscored to the Bundestag that "Islam is part of Germany and part of Europe, it is part of our present and it is part of our future." He identified key issues to be resolved, including the character and location of religious instruction (public schools or Koran schools), the status of women, and the high rates of unemployment. He insists on distinguishing these matters of vital concern to the larger Muslim community from the policies required to respond appropriately to Islamist terrorism, although the public fear that terror evokes makes a clear political separation difficult.

Yet the optimistic conclusion that Muslim identity does not preclude integration becomes less reassuring when one takes into consideration the condition of all immigrants (not only Muslims), numbering some 15 million. Education and employment represent major problems. Approximately 18 percent of children from immigrant families drop out of school, and only 23 percent complete occupational training (compared to 57 percent of Germans). The result is an unemployment rate twice the national average, and considerably lower (79 percent) per capita earnings. It is in this milieu that disaffection with the lack of opportunity can turn into the alienation that is fertile ground for extremism framed in religious terms; in other words, while the older generations, the immigrants themselves, may be less religiously identified—after all, it is they who chose to move to the West—unemployed youth may be susceptible to radical ideologies that appear to draw on religious contents. The path to radicalization involves alienated youth becoming more religious than their nonobservant parents.

According to the Interior Ministry, 12 percent of German Muslims maintain an antidemocratic religious-moral critique of Western society, and 6 percent have an affinity to the use of violence, which represents a significant reservoir for potential radicalization. Yet there is arguably a similarly antidemocratic fringe element in the general population as well; the difference between German fringe elements and immigrant extremism is that for immigrant Muslim youth, radicalized Islam can provide an explanatory narrative for their social marginalization. The core social policy challenge therefore involves understanding this complex entwinement of socioeconomic issues (poor schooling, unemployment) and radical ideology. Both elements play a role. The particularly sensitive challenge is that disaffected youth engaged in juvenile delinquency may invoke ideological predispositions that cannot be neatly segregated from the terms of terrorist Islamism. Of course, juvenile delinquents are not terrorists, but, as elsewhere in Europe, terrorists may recruit from the same alienated cohort that has been socialized to violence and to resentment against German and Western society. This is the recipe for "homegrown" terrorism.

Delinquency and Honor Killings

In an address to the Hanns-Seidl-Stiftung in December 2007, Berlin state attorney Roman Reusch presented a clear, forceful, and controversial articulation of the overlap between urban violence and the Muslim immigrant population. His exposé of failings in the penal, immigration, and judicial systems irritated the political establishment: he was promptly prohibited from accepting an invitation to speak on television, and in less than two months after the initial address, he had been reassigned from an office responsible for repeat offenders— exactly the cohort analyzed in his speech—to a less public desk job, buried deep within the bureaucracy.

In his address Reusch had described the sudden rise in crime rates in immigrant communities during the 1980s, the development of youth violence, and a growing overrepresentation of Arab delinquents. He reported how violent attacks are frequently carried out against Germans, but due to the population concentrations in certain quarters, an increasing number of immigrants have become victims as well. "The victims are generally youth. According to the evidence of the relevant bureau of the Berlin Regional Crime Control Office, youth in Berlin are forty times more like to be a victim of a violent crime than a sixty-year-old. . . . Adults are rarely attacked and typically only when they have a reduced defensive ability, as in the case of the elderly but also of intoxication. Girls and young women . . . are likely to be sexually assaulted, normally accompanied by verbal abuse. . . . These sorts of crimes are marked by an arrogance and contempt on the part

of the perpetrators, rooted in the national-religious sense of
superiority of young Muslim criminals, that becomes particularly offensive toward 'unbelieving' girls and women. The
basic attitude underlying these acts is especially evident in that
the worst accusation against a Muslim girl is that she is acting
like a German. In general, it should be noted that recently the
number of expressly anti-German—and also anti-Jewish—attacks has been increasing."

Because these gangs operate in areas of Berlin in which
the German population has dwindled, they necessarily target
other immigrants, the only available victims. Reusch reports
a typical pattern of Arab delinquents attacking Turkish youth
who are assumed to be less likely to have dropped out of
school. It is a grim picture of a crime-ridden inner city, where
violence against defenseless victims wraps itself in a rhetoric
of religion and extremism, while the local authorities—this is
Reusch's key point—fail to provide the forceful array of responses that might contribute to a reduction in the crime rate:
greater police presence, more severe sentencing guidelines,
and a willingness to initiate deportation proceedings for non-
citizen delinquents.

Juvenile delinquency is also directed against Germans—
especially in and along public transportation routes—but another form of violence explicitly targets vulnerable members
of the immigrant community. At stake here is the phenomenon
of honor killing, when male members of an immigrant family,
steeped in traditionalist expectations about gender roles, strike
out against female family members who seek to take advantage of the opportunities available to women in Western society. While elements of youth crime can be attributed to
socioeconomic circumstances, in particular high unemployment rates, and while the violence can also be understood, in

part, as a response to a sense of ethnic or religious discrimi-nation, there is a further causal component: tensions in gender relations. Whether gender roles are understood in terms of cultural traditions or as the religious mandates of Islam is, at least initially, less important than the sheer fact that male com-munity members react with panic and violence at the pros-pects of female emancipation. In the chapter on England, we saw how the heroine in Monica Ali's *Brick Lane* escaped a traditional marital structure to become independent in London: such is the optimistic version of this transition in family re-lations—there are, unfortunately, plenty of pessimistic ver-sions as well. In Germany, numerous cases of honor killings have been reported in the press, leading to amplified discus-sions around violence tied (correctly or not) to Islam.

The most widely discussed case of honor killing involved the murder of a twenty-three-year-old Turkish-Kurdish wo-man, Hatun Sürücü, gunned down by her brother on February 7, 2005, at a bus stop in the Tempelhof district of Berlin. Her immigrant parents raised her in Germany but sent her back to Turkey at the age of sixteen to enter into an arranged marriage with a cousin. Quickly unhappy in the marriage, she returned to Germany, although she had already become pregnant. She found space in a home for underaged mothers, and was able to complete her high school degree. She eventually found her own apartment and began an apprenticeship as an electrician, which she had nearly completed when she was killed. Her family had resented her efforts to assimilate into German so-ciety by claiming a right to an independent career path and an equally independent social life.

The prosecution attempted to convict her three brothers of having conspired to carry out the killing; the youngest, however, soon confessed, claiming to have acted single-hand-

edly. Observers believe that the whole family had been involved and that the youngest brother confessed only because
the family knew that he would be convicted as a minor and
receive a lesser sentence. In the initial trial the two older
brothers were acquitted, but this was reversed at a higher
level, and a new trial should have taken place. By that time,
however, the two had fled to Turkey, which has refused to
extradite them.

As a high-profile honor killing, the Sürücü murder has
played a role in the debate over the admission of Turkey into
the European Union and also in the public discussion over the
need to achieve a higher degree of cultural integration, including a prohibition of arranged marriages. Women's rights
activists and progressive voices in the Muslim community
have denounced the practice of honor killing; multiculturalists, in contrast, have tried to minimize the importance of the
issue, treating it in terms of varieties of cultural practices and
regarding the public outrage as barely masked nativist animosity to immigrants. For some multiculturalists, any criticism of honor killings amounts to a racist denigration of
immigrants. At the same time, the convicted brother, Ayhan
Sürücü, sentenced to a center for juvenile offenders, has allegedly become a kind of legendary folk idol for young Turks
and Kurds in Germany, regarded with respect and admiration
by his fellow inmates.

That cultural idealization of the masculine avenger of
family honor is indicative, on the one hand, of dynamics in
the immigrant community. Displaced from a traditionalist setting, family members see conventional roles change, in particular, the possibility of greater opportunities for women,
leading to a cultural panic. Some men respond with violence,
be it domestic violence within the family or egregious in-

stances like the Sürücü killing. On the other hand, these eruptions in the microcosm of the family also shed light on a different form of violence, the phenomenon of terrorism in the strict sense: also carried out by young men, acting in desperate rage against the intrusion of Western cultural forms, including changing gender roles. While conventional political debate typically ascribes to terrorists clear and specific political motives, as if they were rational actors carrying out a considered policy, they are surely also driven by fears and anxieties about changing lifestyles. It is an unfortunate failure of interpretation to ascribe to terrorists one-dimensional political or ideological motivations when they are driven, simultaneously, by the same kind of gender panic and lifestyle anxieties that drove the Sürücü brothers to kill their own sister.

Islam, the world religion with more than 4 million adherents in Germany, is not the same as Islamism, a politicized religious discourse driven by an anti-Western animus. Similarly, it is crucial to distinguish between the cultural texture of the Muslim immigrant community, including problematic phenomena such as arranged and forced marriages and honor killings, on the one hand, and, on the other, the security challenges around Islamist terrorism. It makes no sense to suspect the whole immigrant community of terrorist sympathy, nor can one excuse terrorists—such as the Sauerland group—by appealing to the challenges they may have faced as immigrants: many immigrants have faced the same discrimination or economic hardship and nonetheless do not engage in terrorist conspiracies. Still, it remains the case that the cultural contradictions within immigrant culture, exacerbated by the surrounding economic conditions, generate degrees of alienation and disaffection among second- and third-generation immigrants where potential terrorists may be recruited. An international network of jihadist organizations and cells facilitates this recruitment process. Therefore, as much as one needs to separate the questions of immigration from the problem of terrorism on a conceptual level, they interact in complex ways. The debates over immigrant culture are therefore just as much part of the German response to Islamist terrorism as are the controversies surrounding the various counterterrorism policies.

Culture Wars

Just as the history of militarism and dictatorship frames contemporary discussions of German military engagement and counterterrorism, so too does a weighty cultural past intrude on the German debates over immigration and integration. The belated unification of the German nation-state in the nineteenth century had implied a special role for the world of culture—music, literature, philosophy. If Germans did not have a unified state before Bismarck, they at least had a rich world of the arts. This emphatic attachment to high culture as the unifying force of the nation remained the particular paradigm of national self-interpretation throughout the twentieth century: the First World War was waged around the term of *Kultur* and, during the Second World War, it was in culture, especially the culture of exiled authors and intellectuals, many of whom fled to the United States, that a good Germany found refuge during the Hitler years. The question of national culture reemerged abruptly in 1989, when the Berlin Wall fell and Germans, in the West and the East, suddenly had to discover what they might share. Meanwhile, during the process of European unification, which gradually undermines the sovereignty of the individual states, Germany, like its neighbors, has begun to face the need to reexamine the status of national identity and cultural traditions. In that context, especially during the 1990s, a heated debate erupted around citizenship and immigration, particularly driven by the significant influx of refugees, many of them Bosnian Muslims from the wars that ensued when Yugoslavia broke up. In the end, the very restrictive German immigration laws were not revised in any radical way, despite pressure to do so. Still the questions remains: what would it mean to redefine "German identity" in a way that would welcome immigration? How much of German culture should immigrants be required to internalize? Could German society thrive with growing communities of immigrants who hold very different cultural values and have little prospect of integration?

At the beginning of the twenty-first century, therefore, immigration had become a marked topic, as was the national identity of the Germans. In the aftermath of 9/11, the cultural debate over Muslim immigration accelerated, refracted through new paradigms and nuances: the preponderance of Turkish and Turkish-Kurdish immigrant communities, the question of Turkey's entry into the European Union, and the anti-Israel radicalization among Islamists groups, which collided with a German sense of a special post-Holocaust obligation to Israel. If the grandchildren of Nazis labored under a sense of national guilt for Nazi crimes, would that same sensibility transfer to immigrants whose grandparents had been peasants in Anatolia? As traditional progressive notions of universalism and secularism lost ground, multicultural paradigms, often borrowed from the United States, spread. Cultural relativism meant that it was no longer clear that immigrants should be expected to adopt the common culture. This tendency was only amplified by the self-doubt that burdened Germans in light of their past: how could they, of all people, expect foreigners to accept German culture, given its tragic past? If this hesitation was true for immigrants in general, it applied particularly to the many political refugees, especially from the Balkans: surely Germans should not compel them to give up their cultures and to become German. On the contrary, the lessons of multiculturalism mean that Germans should accept and even endorse immigrant diversity.

However noble the principle of tolerance may be, in Germany the deeper ambivalence about national identity was at work. Given their history, Germans were often unwilling to insist on the importance of nationality, and they were certainly unwilling to insist that immigrants become Germans. Yet the German culture of the late twentieth century was hardly the same as the racism and chauvinism of the Nazi era; on the contrary, Germany had become in many ways a "normal" Western European welfare state with secular and progressive values. Nonetheless, there was great reluctance to insist that immigrants from other cultures, especially new arrivals from nonmodern settings, adopt the basic rules of the game of modernity. How can one square the circle of incorporating, for example, a traditionalist and patriarchal set of cultural practices among some immigrant groups with the widely held and legally established norms of equal rights and opportunities?

This challenge set the stage for a German culture war in the middle of the first decade of the new century. As in other European countries, it was modern, secular Muslims—one can think of Salman Rushdie in England or Ayaan Hirsi Ali in the Netherlands—who were in the forefront of a critical discussion of Islam and cultural practices within the immigrant communities. These progressive Muslims, arguing for equal rights and modern norms, found themselves under attack not only by traditionalists and Islamists within the Muslim community, but, almost more disturbingly, by mainstream German intellectuals committed to a multicultural rather than an integrationist agenda. Those advocates of multiculturalism may believe themselves to be well meaning. However, by resisting integration and preserving the separation of immigrant communities from the values and lifestyles of the majority population, they reinforce the culture of separation that generates the resentment and anger that can foster homegrown extremism and enables jihadist recruitment. To undercut the spread of that alienation, integration is the only promising strategy in the long term.

One of the most outspoken advocates of integration, Necla Kelek, was born in Istanbul in 1957 and came to Germany at the age of 11 with her family. Her increasing independence and Westernized attitudes led to conflicts with her parents, who had become gradually more traditionalist and religious. As a professional sociologist, she has turned her attention to the "parallel society" of Turkish immigrants—that is, the immigrant cultural community that has developed in Germany, and alongside Germany, but without significant integration into the German mainstream. Like other Turkish-German feminist authors, such as Seyran Ates, Kelek is a strident critic of the social structures and cultural attitudes that maintain an extreme gender inequality within the immigrant community.

Kelek gained widespread attention with her 2005 book, *The Foreign Bride: A Report from the Interior of Turkish Life in Germany,* which intertwines autobiographical passages with reflections on the deleterious practices and institutions that hamper Turkish assimilation into German society. In particular, Kelek argues against arranged and forced marriages that

typically bring very young and uneducated brides, with no
knowledge of German language and customs, from Turkish
villages to German societies. Not only are the forced marriages abusive to the women, compelling them to accept hus-
bands without any choice, these marital structures also work
against other processes of assimilation of the Turkish minority
into German society by maintaining a large population of uneducated women with no knowledge of the majority language
and therefore trapped within an ethnic ghetto. Otto Schily
praised *The Foreign Bride* in *Der Spiegel,* calling it an
"alarming account" and "an accusation" against forced marriages. "The fundamental obligation to respect other cultural
traditions is limited by the unqualified recognition and applicability of human rights. Forced marriages can under no circumstances be tolerated in a liberal democracy and cannot be
justified on the grounds of cultural or religious traditions. End-
ing this practice is a duty for the whole society—including
both the native and the immigrant populations." *The Foreign
Bride* became a bestseller, and Kelek emerged as a leading
spokesperson for cultural integration; she was appointed to the
Islam Conference organized by the German government, precisely to represent the secular Muslim point of view.

The book won the Geschwister-Scholl-Preis, a literary
prize awarded in Munich named after Sophie and Hans Scholl,
heroes of the anti-Hitler resistance, and given to authors who
demonstrate a spirit of independence, freedom, and courage.
As with Schily's endorsement, the terms of the prize indicate
the stakes with which immigrant culture is being discussed:
Kelek's German admirers associate her work with fundamental issues of human rights and freedom, and the Scholl award
links her symbolically to the highest standard of moral integrity. Just as the Scholls resisted the Nazis, Kelek, by

implication, is doing battle with a new totalitarianism. She fundamentally shifted the discussion about the status of immigrants away from an earlier paradigm, which blamed immigrant suffering on a discriminatory German society, to an account that placed much of the blame on impediments to progress internal to Muslim immigrant cultures, especially its retrograde attitudes toward women, rooted both in traditionalist village life and aspects of Islamic teaching. In that spirit, Kelek's acceptance speech for the Scholl award vividly denounced the processes of isolation and oppression endured by immigrants: "They live in Germany, but according to the rules of an Anatolian village. They have retreated into their faith, their *ummah,* a parallel world; they reproduce it by educating their children the same way they were educated, and they marry them to girls and boys from the old country. This society is in many cases a control system, in which the male elders reign. This is hardly a good precondition for democracy because it would need independent citizens. The failure of integration of so many Turks in Germany has been due, ultimately, to the question of women's emancipation. We have to face this and figure out how we can pull the Muslims out of the ghetto of their parallel society and demand of them an active integration."

Kelek's celebrity and the sudden popularity of other accounts of forced marriages and violence against women, especially personal narratives, quickly provoked an opposition. A public statement entitled "Justice for Muslims!" and signed by sixty German social scientists engaged in research on immigration appeared in the prominent weekly *Die Zeit* on February 2, 2006. The document complained that Kelek and others ascribe to Islam what was in fact a consequence of economic pressures caused, significantly, by restrictive European immigration policies: one of the few remaining ways to enter Europe involves family unification, which encourages the development of a marriage market. More importantly, at stake was a fundamental conflict between strategies of multiculturalism and the desideratum of integration. In particular, the statement complained that so much public attention was being devoted to personal, anecdotal, and even sensationalist texts, when in fact—so the statement asserted—priority should be given to the sort of academic research that the authors of the statement represented. In effect, the scholarly signators were attacking Kelek for writing in a journalistic manner accessible to the wide public sphere, rather than to the closed community of academic professionals. Kelek could therefore easily counter that her opponents were themselves none other than the same academic establishment that, out of a knee-jerk multiculturalism, had promulgated the policies that had been failing for decades and had contributed directly to the emergence of nonintegrated immigrant enclaves.

For Kelek, the critique of Islam as practiced in these immigrant communities is a matter of women's emancipation, democracy, and human rights. Her personal experiences and her training as a sociologist structure her account. A different, if compatible, perspective emerges through the work of another progressive German Muslim, Bassam Tibi. Born in Damascus in 1944, he studied in Germany and became a leading political scientist with a focus on international relations, teaching at the University of Göttingen until his retirement in 2009. A strident critic of Islamism, Tibi argues for a reform of Islam to bring it into the world of enlightened modernity. Any difficulty in distinguishing between Islamism and Islam is due to the fact that the Islamists have successfully disseminated a version of Islam that Tibi regards as deeply distorted. "Political Islam legitimates its resort to violence by reference to an 'Islam under siege,' encircled by 'Jews and Crusaders.' Neither the left nor any other group should tolerate this caricature of Islam, which crudely and propagandistically equates it with Islam. Islam is not Islamism." Tibi could not be more adamant: Islamism, the political discourse that supports terrorism, is not Islam. On the contrary, for Tibi, "Islamism is the most recent and also the most powerful variety of a third-worldist ideology, expressing a new totalitarianism. It is not about liberation." Tibi's perspective betrays his own intellectual socialization within Germany. For him, Islamism, the crucible of terrorist violence, is not a function of Islamic theology at all. On the contrary, it is a late byproduct of the twentieth-century totalitarian movements that still cast a long shadow on European politics. Today's Islamist terrorists, with their disregard for individual lives and liberties and their perverse celebration of redemptive violence, indulge in an extremist culture that inherits more from Nazism and Communism than it does from traditional Muslim faith.

While Kelek finds her adversaries in the multiculturalism of academic social science, Tibi directs his polemic against the political left, which he sees abandoning erstwhile progressive and universal values and instead embracing the deeply unprogressive and illiberal credo of Islamism. Himself identified with the traditions of the European left, Tibi is appalled by the extent to which leftist intellectuals do not merely tolerate the Islam of immigrant culture—as with Kelek's cultural relativist opponents—but also the hardcore jihadist discourses of Islamism. What Tibi identifies is also part of the European response to Islamist terror: the very brutality of the terrorists' violence and their explicit animosity toward the institutions of democratic and capitalist modernity make it, in

the end, uncannily appealing in a twisted way to those parts
of the left who still harbor fantasies of a cataclysmic revolution that would put an end to "bourgeois society." If the opening of the Berlin Wall and the collapse of the Soviet Union
made it clear that no Communist parties would make good on
the images of destruction inherent in their old promises of
revolution, that cultural niche is now occupied by Islamists.
Jihad has taken the place of the "proletarian revolution," and
Islamism is the new Communism precisely because it envisions a similarly repressive order of violence. Tibi carefully
diagnoses how it is Islamism that can be seen as providing a
path to a revolutionary dictatorship, the new caliphate. The
far left happily throws its liberal baggage—human rights,
equal rights, free speech—overboard in order to link up with
the far right in a new totalitarian utopia: Islamo-fascism.

For Tibi, an alternative path is marked by the term he
coined in 1998, *Leitkultur*, the guiding or normative set of
cultural values of society. For Tibi, the term had no national
and certainly no ethnic connotation but rather expressed some
generally Western expectations regarding modernity, in terms
of democracy, secularism, and human rights. Tibi had, in effect, attempted to provide an identity for Europe just as it was
emerging as a newly unified political community: if Europe
were to stand for anything, it should stand for *Leitkultur* as
modernity. Controversy developed, however, when politicians
and journalists began to speak of a specifically German *Leitkultur*, playing it off against multiculturalism and therefore
shading the term toward an ethno-nationalism. Yet the se-
mantics of that dispute are less important than the underlying
principle: would Germany be willing to articulate the expectation that immigrants integrate in the sense of acquiring the
skills to participate in mainstream society—above all German

language skills—and thereby become familiar with the specific rights and responsibilities, and their historical genealogy, that characterize public life in Germany? Or would Germany, hampered by an underlying sense of national guilt, refrain from expecting immigrants to adopt German cultural norms? An integration of the immigrant community into the institutions and norms of democratic Germany could begin to overcome the isolation of the Muslim population and provide its members with the opportunities to succeed in the modern economy. The alternative to the integrationist trajectory is the path toward cultural isolation, nondemocratic values, and the temptations of Islamist terrorism.

One answer to the question—will Germany insist on integration?—has emerged in the "coalition contract," drafted by representatives of the new government parties in the wake of the October 2009 elections. The document, in effect a joint platform, places a premium on integration, beginning with the basics of German language acquisition. "Every child must speak German before beginning school. Therefore we support binding national comparative-standard language tests for all children at the age of four and, when necessary, obligatory preschool language instruction as well as language programs during school." Integration of immigrant families is regarded as a key duty, especially in the wake of the failed multicultural policies of the past: "The deficiencies in integration policies during the past decades must be programmatically overcome. Many people live in our country who, despite years of residency in Germany, are not socially integrated and cannot speak our language. We will support instruments for retroactive integration." Integration and orientation courses—educational opportunities to learn German and to gain familiarity with core aspects of German society (the *Leitkultur* of dem-

ocratic modernity) should be expanded. The new government
advocates a program to open German society to migrant populations, but on terms that are compatible with democratic
German values. Hence the explicit insistence on putting an
end to forced marriages, which is placed on par with slavery:
"Forced marriage is a violation of our liberal democratic value
system and a brazen violation of human rights." Legislation
to criminalize the practice is planned: this is a direct result of
the public discussion that came to a head in response to Kelek's *Foreign Bride*.

The tenor of the coalition contract is, not surprisingly,
conservative and self-assured in its cultural understanding, but
not exclusionary. It identifies the specific contribution religion
can make to social cohesion: "The Christian churches play an
indispensable role in the dissemination of the fundamental
values of our culture. We know that other religions also teach
values that have a positive influence on our society. We respect all religious identities. We have a special responsibility
for the Jewish communities as part of our culture." This af-
firmation of Christianity entails a direct response to the effort
to include a reference to religion in the preamble to the European Constitution, a proposal that faced widespread opposition, especially from secular France. The special responsibility
to Judaism reflects the German past and the Holocaust. Of
particular significance is that, immediately after these references, the document proceeds to declare the intention of the
parties to continue to work with the Islam Conference as a
vehicle for dialogue and integration. Conservative policy involves a balancing act, recognizing the important role religions can play in modern society, while insisting on the centrality of a set of secular, humanistic norms. Where religions
embrace or promote those same norms, all the better.

Finally, the new ruling coalition announces the same combination of assertiveness and openness on a global plane. It designates the engagement in Afghanistan as a "duty of special national interest," because of its contribution to German security, as an expression of solidarity with the people of Afghanistan, and as an indication of German reliability in NATO and the UN. This confirmation of Germany's active posture in Afghanistan coexists with a commitment to a global dialogue with Islam, but the document walks carefully between relativism and universalism. "Societies formed by Islam must find their own paths into modernity and in modernity." In other words, Western standards do not necessarily apply dogmatically everywhere. Nonetheless, "it is in our interest to support the moderate forces striving for democracy and the rule of law." By implication, it will only be through such democratization, a gradual integration of Muslim societies into democratic modernity, that the threat of terrorism can be overcome: "Islamist terrorism is first of all a threat to Muslim societies as well as to us." The diplomacy of the phrasing demonstrates the complexity inherent in the German response to terrorism. It is not a war against Islam, but an effort to cooperate with the Muslim world in order to isolate Islamism. That duality of counterterrorism via cooperation represents, in foreign policy, the corollary to what has been the German domestic response as well: an effort to marginalize xenophobic reactions while pursuing a policy of integration toward immigrant communities in order to enhance their participation in German society and thereby reduce the appeal of terrorist recruiting.

This is a multipronged strategy facing a set of complex challenges. To preserve security, Germany has benefited from political leaders, like Schily and Schäuble, who have advocated effectively for strong counterterrorism measures. To promote integration, the contributions of intellectuals and writers like Kelek and Tibi have been crucial. To contribute to the international order, Germany has overcome its post–World War II pacifist inclinations and contributes, albeit in a moderate way, to ISAF. If its totalitarian past makes Germany apprehensive in terms of military participation or counterterrorist police powers, that same past also enables Germans, who have built a successful liberal democratic state, to understand the importance of resisting and defeating a movement of extremist terror that is a dedicated enemy of free societies.

CHAPTER FIVE

Belgium, Holland, Denmark

Terror in Small Nations

In the three preceding chapters, we have examined the responses to terrorism and Islamism in the context of larger issues of immigration in three of the major countries of Western Europe, each with its own distinctive history and cultural traditions. In England, the response to Islamism is framed by the history of empire, the experience of immigration from former colonies, and the memories of terrorism associated with the dispute over Northern Ireland. France carries a similar history of colonialism, burdened by recollections of the special brutality of the Algerian war, but the problem of terror also resonates with the national memory of revolution. The legacy of the French Revolution is thoroughly intertwined with an adamant secularism, as suspicion of religion that derives from the eighteenth-century enlightenment, and the civic ethos of republicanism—the priority of civic virtue, citizenship and loyalty to the state, over membership in any ethnic or religious community. In England, as we saw, an important discussion has ensued about a potential role for Muslim religious law, sharia, in the public sphere, and this discussion has been spearheaded by none other than the head of the Anglican Church. In France, the issue is not the encounter between different religions, but the distinction between secularism and religion as such.

Germany, meanwhile, approaches these matters in different ways altogether. Unlike France, Germany is not predisposed to resent religion as such; and unlike England, there is no single, hegemonic religion—this is the country of the Reformation after all—which has implied some room for diversity of different faiths. However, Germany's political history—the legacy of the Second World War and the Holocaust—still weighs heavily on the national consciousness: hence both a reluctance to be critical of minority religions or ethnicities, but also a discomfort with the volatile mixture of anti-Zionism and anti-Semitism that pervade Islamism. Often reluctant to display national pride or self-confidence, many Germans feel unwilling to be seen as judging foreign customs, which sends them sliding down the slippery slope of a postmodern cultural relativism. Defense of universal values ends up in the hands of progressive Muslim intellectuals who face opponents on many fronts: traditional Muslims, Islamist radicals, multicultural relativists and the hardcore leftists who have inherited the mantle of the otherwise discredited Communist past.

We now turn to three smaller countries, each an important European landscape, to be sure, but each a much smaller and perhaps therefore more tightly knit culture. The classic modernist author, Franz Kafka—a German-speaking Jew who lived in Prague among a Czech population when the city was part of the transnational Austro-Hungarian Empire—once commented on the literatures of "small nations," in which he finds greater vibrancy and shared participation in cultural matters than in the larger and (he assumes) more bureaucratic countries. Citizens of small countries may have some greater cosmopolitanism, since they have to learn other "world languages" in order to travel abroad, but they may also maintain a strong local sense of cultural and linguistic identities, since their communities are so small. This dynamic may explain why some of the most complex and volatile conflicts around Islamism and Muslim immigration have taken place in smaller countries—Belgium, the Netherlands, and Denmark.

Stretched along the northern coast of continental Europe, these countries all have their own distinctiveness. Belgium is itself a country of two languages and cultures, French and Flemish, and the often French-speaking North African immigrants have at times exacerbated local language conflicts. Netherlands and Denmark enjoyed, until recently, a reputation of extraordinary tolerance supported by generous social-welfare networks. While everywhere many immigrants strive to take advantage of the opportunities afforded them and to integrate—reminiscent of the optimistic narrative of immigration in *Brick Lane*—this has not always been the case, and ghettoized subcultures have developed. In addition to the standard social problems of disadvantaged communities, Islamist radicalism has festered and exploited the disaffections of immigrant life. As public attention has begun to recognize this threat, especially in the wake of some uniquely dramatic events, opinion has moved away from the naïvely multiculturalist agenda of the past toward cultural policies focused more on preserving the integrity of national identity and traditions. Needless to say, this turn has not been without controversy; the advocates of multiculturalism—the opponents of local European traditions, but simultaneously the paternalistic advocates of immigrant cultures—are numerous and well placed. Still, the tide has begun to turn.

Belgium

On November 9, 2005, an American soldier on patrol in Baquba, Iraq, was wounded in an attack carried out by a suicide bomber. The event was distinctive because the perpetrator, Muriel Degauque, a Belgian convert to Islam, may have been the first European woman to carry out such an attack. In some ways, hers was the unique story of a troubled individual: despite a normal childhood, she fell into drug use as a teenager, lost her brother in a motorcycle accident, and briefly married an older Turkish man in what may have just been a strategy to legalize his status. Her second husband, from Algeria, introduced her to Islam, which she embraced with growing fervor. According to Belgian police, the husband was connected to a group associated with Abu Musab al-Zarqawi, intent on recruiting European fighters for jihad. Some terrorist experts took her case to be indicative of the growing potential for Europeans, and especially European women, to be drawn into terrorist networks and to end up carrying out jihadist violence. French antiterrorism officials had been warning for years that female converts to Islam represented a growing threat. To be sure, conversion is not a crime; some conversions are sincere expressions of belief, even if many take place pro forma to satisfy the bride's or groom's traditionalist parents or to obtain citizenship. In Degauque's case, however, a labile personality probably found the rigor of fundamentalism appealing in a way that led her, perhaps through manipulation, to her death in a suicide bombing. The moderate Muslim Belgian journalist Hind Fraihi took Degauque's sorry fate as grounds to warn that "the seeds of terror have been sown throughout the world, even in Belgium."

Soon after the Degauque attack, on January 26, 2006, Belgian police searched seventeen houses in Brussels associated with extremist Islamism, including the Centre Islamique Belge (CIB), located in the Molenbeek section of Brussels, a heavily immigrant quarter. The head of the CIB, Bassam Ayachi, was a native Syrian with French citizenship who had been living in Molenbeek for years. A Salafist preacher, he was closely connected to Abdessatar Dahmane, who took part in the September 9, 2001, suicide attack that killed Ahmed Shah Massoud, the leader of the Afghan Northern Alliance and an opponent of the Taliban and of Osama bin Laden. That assassination has been construed as a "gift" to bin Laden on the eve of the attacks in New York and Washington, and the paths to it lead through Brussels.

Moreover, Ayachi published a notorious letter, posted on the Internet, dated January 1, 2004, directed to the then French interior minister and entitled "When Death Becomes Beautiful, Monsieur Sarkozy." The primary theme of the document is the willingness to die for faith, "the logic of Muslims, when their path is blocked . . . with no exit and not the least light giving even the tiniest of hope of escaping. At that moment, throwing oneself toward death becomes something beautiful, in the same way we find in the image of moths rushing by the hundreds toward the gleaming light, without worrying about the heat of the lamp that will burn them; on the contrary, they would rather die burning in the center of the light than to stay in the darkness." Ayachi's complaint to Sarkozy does not involve the headscarf dispute which, in January 2004, was only beginning to develop, but rather the interior minister's efforts to establish an official Muslim council in France (comparable to the official representation of other religions and parallel to the Muslim Council in Germany) in order for the government to have a clear and official interlocutor in the Islamic community. Yet Ayachi objects to Sarkozy's outreach to centrist Muslim leaders, and he predicts that the whole initiative will fail, at which point his rhetoric takes on a threatening tone: "at that moment the moths will jump into the light and fall into the flames without worrying about death in order to save themselves from the darkness. . . . And that's when death will become beautiful, Monsieur Sarkozy, interior minister of France! I share with you my concern and fear that this will happen."

The letter couches this objection to Sarkozy's policy of outreach in a framework of the larger jihadist vision—hostility to Zionism, denunciation of the Russians in Chechnya, and animosity to the United States—all interwoven with quotations from the Koran. That was in 2004. Ayachi escaped the January 2006 raid on CIB in Brussels, but by 2009 he was being held by Italian authorities in Bari on charges of organizing illegal immigration, when he was charged additionally with planning a terrorist attack against Charles De Gaulle airport in Paris. According to ABC News, he was suspected of being one of the key Al Qaeda agents in Europe.

Islamist extremism had clearly succeeded in finding a secure home in Brussels, and it was therefore with a visit to Ayachi at the CIB that the journalist Hind Fraihi, working undercover and claiming to be a student of sociology, began her investigation of radicalism in Molenbeek in 2006. As a document, her *Infiltré parmi les radicaux islamistes* (Infiltrated: among radical Islamists) is comparable to other examples of journalism by disguise—the American classic *Black Like Me*, or, in Germany, Günter Wallraff's account of the

condition of Turkish migrant labor, *Ganz Unten*. Like those
other examples of reportage by deception, Fraihi's volume
bears the same ethical flaw: the reporter pretended to be someone she was not in order to elicit revealing statements from
the residents of Molenbeek. Yet more importantly—and
thanks to this deception—her writing is a revealing exposé of
immigrant life and therefore a piece of enlightenment. It is
exemplary investigative journalism that shows to the public—
and first of all to the Belgian public—the way extremism can
thrive in its midst, with advocates of jihad calling for violence
while trying to recruit disoriented youth as foot soldiers in
their warfare against free societies. However, Fraihi's inquiry
by no means amounts to a black and white simplification of
the ideological conflicts among Muslim immigrants in Belgium, and it is certainly not a crude binary account, counter-
posing Muslim immigrants against native Belgians. On the
contrary, her description includes a nuanced portrait of a society in which largely Moroccan immigrants and their offspring pursue numerous and diverse paths of socialization in
Molenbeek, with a cast of characters ranging from radicals
like Ayachi to moderate and even conservative immigrants,
who have come to identify with Belgium, who are grateful
for the opportunities afforded to them, who are proud of their
own accomplishments, and who therefore emphatically reject
Islamist extremism.

Herself the daughter of affluent Moroccan immigrants,
Fraihi was engaged by the Belgian daily *Nieuwsblad* to spend
two months in Molenbeek to explore the scope of Islamist
extremism in Belgium and to evaluate the likelihood of terrorist attacks. Her investigation included attendance at radical
mosques as well as interviews with disaffected youth, and her
account contextualizes her findings with her own autobio-

graphical familiarity with Belgian Islam. In the face of the
severe strictures of fundamentalism that she finds in the
mosques and especially the rules regulating women's lives,
Fraihi insists on recalling the open and tolerant Islam with
which she had grown up. Jihadist world conquest "is not the
Islam I know, or rather, it is not Islam at all. I was educated
in a peaceful and tolerant religion: no war, no deaths, yes to
liberty and welcoming joy. An anarchist religion with a bit of
flower power—that is my Islam." But in Molenbeek she finds
instead an overwhelming focus on war, on the one hand, and
the repressive lifestyles, especially for women, on the other.
Why, she asks, does the Islamist politicization of religion and
the turn toward neotraditionalist lifestyles proliferate in sectors of the immigrant community?

Fraihi points out that severe Islamist doctrine is disseminated in part through Saudi-funded networks of preaching and
publications that promote the Wahabi version of the faith.
Their impact, however, is more complex, a function of deeper
cultural processes within the immigrant community and its
interaction with Belgian society. Fraihi can touchingly recall
her childhood friend, Sahar, once a thoroughly Westernized
young woman, whom she discovers to have turned to Muslim
traditionalism and traditionalist fashion: "Loosely fitting pants
and blouse. Nothing close to the body, everything in dark
beige. She wears flat shoes, some orthopedic type, not at all
fashionable. And to recall how you could hear her coming
from far away, walking quickly in her high heels. What a
change!" Fraihi speculates that this severe transformation represents ultimately a kind of protest gesture—she calls it "Muslim punk," an ostentatious rejection of the host culture, but at
the same time remarkably similar to protest gestures in the
"no future" generation of European youth more broadly.

While the turn to a stringent Islam may invoke traditionalist teachings and quotations from the Koran, it does not derive simply from religious instruction. On the contrary, for
Fraihi it represents a response to the values crisis of Belgian
society: because the host society has no clear values identity,
alienated immigrant youth turn to an ultraorthodox version of
their own heritage. According to Fraihi, therefore, one should
not attribute this neotraditionalism solely to the socioeconomic disadvantage in immigrant communities, since it appeals to the younger generation in the Muslim middle classes
as much as it does to unemployed youth. Certainly, Saudi
pamphlets and propaganda play a role, as do the social conditions of the poorer strata. Yet the phenomenon has to be
evaluated in the cultural context of contemporary Europe: "Is
it a form of protest against (post)-modernity? Is it the romantic
side of religion that is so attractive to Sahar? Is she on a search
for her 'grand narrative,' for her epic? Like the British appealing to King Arthur and the masses of youth who find parts
of their identity in films like *The Lord of the Rings*? Is she
looking for happiness in simplicity? Is puritan Islam her
escape?"

Yet while some, like Sahar, turn to ultra-traditionalist lifestyles in a search for meaning in the modern world, others
insist on the values of modernity. Fraihi reports on immigrants—often older, successful, and integrated—who speak
proudly of their positive immigrant experience and who value
their lives in Belgium. From their point of view, the radicalization of the younger generation is a function of the permissiveness of Belgian society: in other words, even though the
young radicals adopt a neo-Islamic idiom (to which the Wahabi network and jihadist propaganda welcome them eagerly),
they are products of a Belgian society unsure of itself and

therefore all too willing to broadcast a cultural relativist multiculturalism. That this politically conservative criticism of multiculturalism emerges from within the immigrant community is noteworthy and constitutes a key piece of Fraihi's account. It is these pro-Western immigrants who are particularly sensitive to the increasingly repressive cultural atmosphere within the Belgian Muslim community. "I never wore a headscarf in Morocco, and I have no intention of wearing one here," reports Fatima, who had immigrated to Belgium and blames many of the problems on the generations born in Belgium. While she wants to insist on her own modern lifestyle, she reports facing harassment in Molenbeek: "Now when I go outside without a head covering, some Muslim extremists call me immoral." Fatima's account involves one of the paradoxes of immigration in the age of multiculturalism: she left Morocco in the pursuit of modernity, but she now faces experiences in Belgium less modern and more repressive than the Morocco she left behind.

Contemporary Europe appears to betray the promise of modernity—individual freedom and economic opportunity—that it once represented. Instead its permissiveness turns into a hothouse for radical antimodernism. No wonder Fatima complains: "We moderate Muslims are the first victims of the Muslim extremists. . . . But no one defends us. The Belgian authorities are too permissive, and the Muslim organizations only condemn Flemish extremism, while giving free rein to the extremists in our own community." Fraihi therefore identifies a tendency in parts of the immigrant community to move politically to the right, even to the Flemish nationalist Vlams Belang Party, and in any case away from the stereotypical association of immigrants with the center-left, which she caricatures with the designation "Islamosocialism."

In this complex universe of Molenbeek, Fraihi encounters competing agendas: Ayachi's jihadist extremism linked to networks of terror, Sahar's demonstratively antimodern neo-traditionalism, and Fatima's immigrant optimism, a proudly conservative modernism. In this heterogeneous world, she also finds fertile soil for propaganda: unemployed and disaffected youth, supported by the social-welfare system but cynical about the established order. Their juvenile delinquency in violent encounters with the Brussels police merges all too quickly with images of war from Iraq and Afghanistan, and they talk casually about suicide attacks, just as they also report on obscure efforts to recruit them for jihad. The social alienation of segregated existence in the Molenbeek ghetto lends itself to the radical interpretations provided by professional extremists like Ayachi or disseminated on ubiquitously available television channels from the Middle East, not to mention the jihadist temptations of the Internet.

Meanwhile the semiofficial multiculturalism of Belgian society systematically refrains from offering positive counternarratives of integration and modernization. The various voices of Muslim modernization who appear in Fraihi's account confess their exasperation that there are so few allies in the war of ideas against radicalization. Fraihi herself concludes her book with an exhortation to the Belgian public that an open discussion about the ominous slide toward extremism is urgently needed. As long as the floor is ceded to radicals, it is not surprising that the most radical interpretations—Fraihi would say "misinterpretations"—of Islam circulate and find adherents among individuals estranged from society and who, for whatever reasons, see little opportunity for their futures. It is they who could succumb to Ayachi's appeal to the beauty of death. Without positive prospects for Molenbeek, Islamist terrorism may remain appealing enough to lead the disaffected to violence.

The Netherlands

Holland is similar in many ways to its neighbor Belgium: a geographically small country but an important member of the Western European community. Like Belgium, it was once a major colonial power, although Dutch colonialism began much earlier and led, ultimately, to extensive immigration from former colonies, especially Indonesia, which has influenced the texture of society and culture. A sense of guilt from the colonial age as well as from the extensive Dutch collaboration with the German occupation in the Second World War still plays a role in the national self-understanding. Holland is the country where Anne Frank hid and where Dutch neighbors betrayed her to the Nazis. As a reaction against that past, the Netherlands, especially since the early 1960s, has tried to reinvent itself as a bastion of progressive culture, the quintessentially tolerant European welfare state. Holland was, after all, one of the homelands of the European enlightenment and parliamentary government. The trajectory of cultural development in Holland is, arguably, a litmus test for the potentials of the enlightenment legacy in the twenty-first century.

Despite Dutch aspirations to engineer the perfect society, things began to sour. The catastrophic role played by the Dutch military, under United Nations command, in Srebrenica in 1995 traumatized the nation: their soldiers had been forced to stand by helplessly while thousands of Bosnian Muslims refugees, who had tried to seek the protection of Dutch soldiers, were handed over to Serb forces, where they were quickly slaughtered. This inability to prevent genocide—or rather, this participation in the structure of international governance, the UN, which proved itself woefully inadequate to the task—undermined the earlier self-confidence of progressive Holland and liberal Europe in general. The massacre at Srebrenica left a deep scar in Dutch identity that genocide could happen again on European soil, all sanctimonious assurances to the contrary notwithstanding. Moreover, the Dutch had been front and center in the inability to prevent this new evil. One cannot underestimate the gravity of this trauma. If there was any consensus in democratic Western Europe after World War II, it was that Auschwitz, as a metaphor for any genocide, should not happen again. But then came Srebrenica, and the Dutch stood by as if another betrayal of Anne Frank were taking place.

The Bosnian catastrophe challenged the Dutch in another, very specific way. While their failure in the Balkans made them focus on Muslims as victims, cultural tendencies in the Muslim immigrant community in Holland raised other issues. The Dutch stereotypically prided themselves on their social liberalism—German women could travel to Holland for abortions forbidden in their home country, permissive drug laws made Dutch cities havens for marijuana tourists, and Holland become famous for its acceptance of homosexual lifestyles. As early as 1996, gay couples could register their partnerships and receive rights comparable to those accorded married couples, and in 2000 the Netherlands became the first country to grant official recognition to marriages of same-sex couples. Yet this capacious tolerance which, for the Dutch, seemed to be cut from the same cloth as their readiness to welcome immigrants from other cultures, sowed the seeds for a profound cultural conflict—for many of the North African Muslim immigrants settling in Holland held much more traditionalist attitudes at odds with the permissive hedonism of northern Europe.

Reports of homophobic attacks by immigrant youth began to circulate as did accounts of brutal mistreatment of women in parts of the immigrant community—arranged marriages, female genital mutilation, exclusion from education, repressive living conditions, and more. Liberal Holland began to face the classical paradox of liberalism: if the country was to accord equal rights to immigrants, was it also obliged to enforce its own expectations of equality even within the immigrant community? If it would live by the rules of tolerance, what stance should it adopt toward apparent intolerance? And in light of its own shame over the role too many Dutch had played in collaborating with the Nazis and contributing to the Holocaust, how could Holland address the circulation of anti-Jewish sentiment among Muslim immigrants? Given Holland's deep roots in the enlightenment tradition and given its pronounced liberal self-understanding, it is not surprising that it was explicitly and foremost in this country that some intellectuals, both native Dutch and immigrants to the Netherlands, addressed some of the underlying conceptual problems head-on, especially in the tense atmosphere after the September 11 attacks.

As we have seen, some of the most powerful criticism of Muslim extremism comes from other Muslims. Born in Tehran in 1966, Afshin Ellian fled the Iranian revolution, eventually arriving in the Netherlands in 1989, where he studied law and philosophy, completed a doctorate with a dissertation on the South African Truth and Reconciliation Commission, and became a professor of law at the University of Leiden. For Ellian, the defense of the secular character of the modern state is crucial; while the insistence on the separation between religion and politics does not imply hostility to religion, it does mean refusing the agenda of any particular religion to exercise political power. He therefore examines how different religions understand politics.

According to Ellian, a separation of political and religious spheres emerges at the very origins of Christianity and continues into the Middle Ages in the form of the competition between emperor and pope. Islam, however, is another matter. In particular, Ellian identifies the conflation of the original Muslim war against polytheist religions with Mohammed's own aspirations to political power. It is this politicized pursuit of dogmatic monotheism, at the outset of Islam, which, he claims, makes discussions of Islam so difficult. This intrusion of politics into religion also generates a profoundly repressive political program—not for individual Muslims but for politicized Islam. "Islam has always had two faces: a political one and a mystical one. For most Muslims the practices of Islam are merely habitual, but because of the fact that the prophet Mohammed—and not the Imams—laid the foundation for political Islam (alongside mystical Islam), it has become impossible to pose critical political questions without touching upon essential elements of Islam." On the one hand, this connection to the core of Islam makes discussion difficult and controversial; on the other, it generates a tendency in politicized Islam—which is not the Islam that most Muslims live—toward an all-encompassing and totalizing program, with ominous consequences: "Political Islam is a totalitarian movement and an enemy of Muslims and non-Muslims alike."

To be clear: Ellian's accusation is not directed at Muslims, whom he sees living their faith in many diverse and nonrepressive ways, nor is it directed at Islam as a set of doctrines and teachings, but at the Islamist effort to transform religion directly into politics, which threatens the foundation of the modern civil state. To avoid this danger, Islam, so Ellian argues, has to submit to a process of modernizing enlightenment, the same process that led to the secularization of Europe and produced the institutions of Dutch society. "Just as Christianity has submitted to the rules of the open society and the liberal state, so too could Islam accept these same rules."

Ellian's philosophical response to Islamism entails a call for enlightenment within Islam. It is also an appeal for the defense of secular political structures—exactly the secularism that was lost to politics in the Khomeinist Iran that he had to flee. It is only consistent that he insists on the urgency of the battle for human rights in the Islamic world, and at the center of the pursuit of rights he places women's rights. A kindred spirit, another Muslim immigrant to Holland, Ayaan Hirsi Ali, has lived that struggle for gender equality in Islam. Born in 1969 in Somalia, her family emigrated to Kenya, Saudi Arabia (where she first encountered Islam as a severe religion), and Ethiopia. In 1992 she traveled to Europe. Her family intended that she proceed to Canada to enter a marriage to a cousin arranged by her father, but instead, in order to avoid the marriage, she sought and was granted political asylum in Holland. She was eventually able to attend university while working as a Somali-Dutch interpreter, which brought her into contact with women seeking asylum or safety from domestic violence. Her own experience and her interaction with the social service network provided her extensive opportunity to observe the operations of Dutch social agencies and the plight of women in the immigrant community, including their mistreatment and the reluctance of the Dutch to criticize conditions among immigrants. Behind that hesitation Hirsi Ali identified a lack of self-confidence in Dutch cultural identity. One anecdote makes that mentality abundantly clear. On the day she received Dutch citizenship in 1997, she was stunned that her friends reacted with cold dismissiveness: "my Dutch friends seemed uncomfortable with the symbols of Dutchness: the flag and the monarchy. These things seemed to them to hark back to the treacherous days of the Second World War. They saw nationalism as almost the same thing as racism. Nobody seemed *proud* of being Dutch."

Ali gradually gained entrance into Dutch political circles, initially around the center-left Labor Party, but she felt disaffected with its reluctance to criticize the shortcomings of multicultural policies. Her own stance was shifting as well; through a profound crisis of conscience she broke not only with Islam, but with religion in general and declared herself to be an atheist. This development led her, however, to even more pronounced public criticisms of problems, and not only in the Muslim community: for example, she attacked funding for religious schools in general—much of Dutch education takes place in Catholic and Protestant schools—but she reserved her primary attention to the mistreatment of women in Muslim communities. For her, the problem facing Holland was not simply Islamism (the politicized movement around Islam) but a much wider set of cultural practices frequently associated with Islam, or at least with the forms of Islam that had migrated from Northern Africa to Europe. Her positions found resonance in the center-right Liberal Party, with which she affiliated, and she would soon join its caucus in the Dutch parliament. Yet precisely while she was beginning to gain this success in the Dutch political sphere, she increasingly became the target of attacks and even death threats for her public critiques of Islam.

The controversy around Hirsi Ali came to a head in the

wake of the assassination of her friend and collaborator, the artist and filmmaker Theo van Gogh, discussed below. The assassin left a note threatening her as well. Hirsi Ali had to go into hiding, under police protection, and eventually fled Holland for the United States. Subsequently, her public image was tarnished by doubts regarding the terms on which she had initially applied for asylum, and an extensive political controversy ensued. She had apparently used a false name in her original asylum application—a stratagem designed to help her escape the members of her family intent on pushing her into an arranged marriage. Her Dutch political opponents took full advantage of this problem in order to undermine her integrity and reputation. This problem should not, however, overshadow the crux of the matter: Hirsi Ali's consistently vocal criticism of patriarchal structures in Islam, the systematic subordination of women—which is the subject of the film, *Submission,* on which she had collaborated with van Gogh—and the urgent need for the Dutch state to maintain the same standards for women's rights and equality within the immigrant community on which it would insist for the rest of the Dutch population. Hirsi Ali's multiculturalist opponents were trying to deflect attention from these matters by using her asylum application problem as a pretext.

It is ironic that the political debate around Hirsi Ali eventually involved the question of whether the state would provide her police protection from the Islamist extremists who had threatened her life. Her critique of multiculturalism and her public advocacy had consistently underscored the unwillingness of the Dutch state to defend the equal rights of Muslim women. Now her own life was threatened, and many begrudged her the police protection she received. Dutch opinion was divided; while there were certainly many who supported the protection in order to stand with her to defend her right to speak, considerable currents in progressive Holland were, basically, irritated that her advocacy for women's rights ran the risk of disrupting the peaceful normalcy of their everyday life. Why, after all, should they be asked to bear the costs of defending freedom? Why stand up for principles that might irritate the extremists? A psychology of appeasement was at work that was prepared to forego freedom in order to avoid conflict. Her autobiography, published as *Infidel* in English (highlighting the clash of religions), in fact bears a Dutch title that means "My Freedom." It is this freedom that the Dutch preferred not to defend.

Similarly, her exodus from Somalia to the West was, in her eyes, a journey toward freedom, and her life work involves its defense. Her collection of essays on women in Islam, *The Caged Virgin*, similarly bears a bold subtitle: *An Emancipation Proclamation for Women and Islam*. If there is a moral to her story, it is that the progressive European public cannot be counted on to stand firmly behind the agenda of women's rights if it stirs up trouble or runs counter to the precepts of multiculturalism. The universalism of rights is not compatible with the paradigm of cultural relativism, and it is here, in this unwillingness to defend values that contemporary European culture shows its greatest vulnerability in its confrontation with Islamist reaction.

The character of this reaction is nowhere more evident than in the assassination of Theo van Gogh (his great grandfather was the brother of the famous painter Vincent van Gogh). Born in 1947 into a prominent family in the Dutch cultural world, he built a career as a cultural critic, film director, and general gadfly, taking many controversial positions. Hostile to all religion, he emerged as a strident critic of

Islam, which he saw as propagating values antithetical to Holland's open society. He supported Hirsi Ali's candidacy for the parliament, and he collaborated with her on a film, *Submission,* a short avant-garde treatment of misogyny in the Koran. It was broadcast on Dutch television in August 2004. On November 2, Mohammed Bouyeri, a twenty-six-year-old Dutch-Moroccan, stabbed and killed van Gogh as he was bicycling to work in Amsterdam. After attempting to behead van Gogh, Bouyeri left a note justifying the killing on Islamist grounds, pinned to the body with two knives. Apprehended and convicted, Bouyeri, who had ties to the terrorist network the Hofstad group, is currently serving a life sentence with no chance of parole.

The van Gogh assassination shocked the Dutch public, coming on the heels of the 2002 assassination of the maverick politician Pim Fortuyn, who had also criticized Islam and advocated restrictions on immigration. The peaceful self-understanding of Holland was shaken to the core, and the network of problems around Islamism and immigration were moving to the center of national consciousness. Yet the reality of Holland is not just its progressivism; it is also the Islamist subculture that has thrived in its midst, and for which Bouyeri provides ample evidence. In the open letter to Hirsi Ali that the assassin pinned to van Gogh's corpse, Bouyeri indulges in apocalyptic and anti-Semitic visions (neither Hirsi Ali nor van Gogh was Jewish), and he promises the destruction of America, Europe, Holland, and Hirsi Ali. In another document that he carried with him and which indicated that he had intended to die as a martyr in the attack, he invokes imagery of death, both as a threat to his opponents and as the eschatological framework for Islamist politics: "To the enemy I also have something to say . . . You will certainly try to resist

. . . But even if you go on a tour of the world . . . Death is lurking right behind you . . . The horsemen of death are at your heels . . . And the streets will be covered red with blood." He insisted on the duty of Muslim warriors to kill nonbelievers; "It is undisputed that the blood of a *Kafir* (infidel) is *halal* (allowed). So it is written in the law, no one can disagree about that. . . . Islam has come to submit the lie and the adherents of the lie to the truth, if necessary by the sword."

This scenery of destruction and religious warfare coexists for Bouyeri with an imagined triumph of Islamism, as he wrote elsewhere: "By the grace of Allah, a generation will rise that will use death with their own blood and their own souls as a shield around our *Umma*. It is a question of time before the knights of Allah will march into the Binnenhof [Dutch parliament] in the Hague to raise the flag of Tawheed. They will *(insha'Allah)* change the parliament into a Sharia court, the chairman's hammer will go down to ratify the Islamic sentences, the gong will spread the Islamic law over the rest of the Netherlands like the ripples from a drop. From the tower of Kok [referring to the private office of the prime minister] we'll hear *(insha'Allah) La ilaha illa Allah*." For Bouyeri's Islamist vision, a straight line leads from the violence against critics of Islam like Hirsi Ali and van Gogh to the establishment of an Islamist regime in Holland. Islam and Islamism tend to collapse into one, as religion and politics merge, and the religious pursuit of the rule of a single faith becomes, as Ellian describes, an agenda for a totalitarian regime. The complicated texture of issues that we saw in Fraihi's account of Molenbeek—juvenile delinquency, immigration assimilation or separation, the status of women in immigrant families, postmodern values in the West—suddenly disappear in apocalyptic political fantasies.

Denmark

The post–9/11 years witnessed a rise in anti-Americanism that targeted the foreign policy of the Bush administration, especially the wars in Afghanistan and Iraq, while public opinion across Europe seemed to verge to the left. Yet one of the noticeable paradoxes of the era is that, on the national level, many European countries have witnessed a conservative ascendancy. This was certainly the case in Denmark—one of the paragons of the Scandinavian welfare-state model, it elected a right-wing government in 2001, indicative of a gradual rightward drift, especially in northern Europe. Part of this shift can be attributed to the social and cultural impact of immigration and the cultural conflicts ensuing from large Muslim populations, especially in the otherwise largely homogenous societies of Scandinavia.

The terms of cultural policy also began to shift, from an advocacy for an elitist modernism in the name of cultural democracy to a rediscovery of national identity and the importance of national canons of great works. Late in 2004, the conservative Danish minister of cultural affairs, Brian Mikkelsen, for example, defined an "initiative to articulate and present what he termed a 'national cultural canon,' including the best works of art ever created in Danish culture." This was hardly noncontroversial: the stage was set for conflict, a culture war between radicalism and conservatism, between proponents of multiculturalism and those who understood the value of a national identity.

Against this background, the events in the Netherlands unleashed an important ripple effect. The assassination of Theo van Gogh in November 2004 was taken as Bouyeri intended it to be taken: a warning to Europe to refrain from expressing any criticisms of Islam or Islamism (whereby the two terms, which Fraihi tries to keep apart, began to draw closer together). Even before the Amsterdam killing, a disturbing event took place that received widespread attention in Denmark: in October, a lecturer at the University of Copenhagen who had quoted from the Koran during a class was physically attacked by a group of assailants. They objected precisely to a non-Muslim citing the Koran in public. Would Danish intellectuals begin to censor themselves on topics concerning Islam? And would this self-censorship begin to generate a less intellectually vibrant, more repressive cultural atmosphere? The newspaper *Politiken* reported how the author of a children's book on the life of Mohammed had faced difficulties finding an illustrator for the volume: artists felt that contributing depictions of Mohammed might offend Muslims and lead to harassment or violence. The local liberalism of Denmark was coming under the pressure of the illiberalism of other cultures in the context of globalization.

Some of the anxiety among Danish artists stemmed from a misunderstanding of the Islamic injunction against pictorial images, and some from a cautious reluctance to become involved in anything related to Islam. In order to sharpen the discussion on this matter, the daily *Jyllands-Posten* published, on September 30, 2005, twelve drawings or cartoons (in the sense of political cartoons) on or related to Mohammed. The intent was to provoke a discussion about self-censorship, but also to satirize: the excessive piety directed toward Islam, the fear of reprisals, multicultural sanctimony, and the artists themselves. As the editor of *Jyllands-Posten* later explained to the *Washington Post*: "the cartoonists treated Islam the same way they treat Christianity, Buddhism, Hinduism, and other religions. And by treating Muslims in Denmark as equals they made a point: We are integrating you into the Danish tradition of satire because you are part of our society, not strangers. The cartoons are including, rather than excluding, Muslims."

Protests against the publication began immediately upon their publication, in Denmark and then overseas. This reaction, however, was relatively constrained and might have subsided until, after some time, matters escalated when a group of Danish imams toured the Middle East. They carried with them a dossier containing the cartoons and other documents to demonstrate the allegedly beleaguered state of Muslims in Denmark. The dossier also included hate mail allegedly received by Danish Muslims, as well as other images that were not among the cartoons published by *Jyllands-Posten*—some of these supplementary images had nothing at all to do with Islam but, misunderstood as hostile gestures, they fanned the flames. Demonstrations took place across the Muslim world: Danish embassies were burned, other European buildings attacked, and nearly one hundred deaths occurred. A boycott of Danish goods took place, leading to a significant impact on Danish trade.

The reprinting of the cartoons in other European newspapers—as a sign of solidarity with the principle of a free press—spread the protests as well. In Berlin, police subdued a Pakistani student who had entered the offices of the newspaper *Die Weit* armed with a knife and who admitted to planning to kill its editor. (The student, Amer Cheema, later killed himself in prison; his family claims he was tortured, and his funeral in Lahore in 2006 attracted tens of thousands.) The aftershocks of the affair would continue: in February 2008, Danish police arrested a group of men allegedly planning to assassinate Kurt Westergaard, the illustrator of the one cartoon images that integrated a bomb into a turban, while as recently as January 1, 2010, Westergaard faced an intruder armed with an axe and shouting for "revenge." (The suspect was arrested and identified as a Somali with links to Al Qaeda.) Moreover, when Yale University Press planned a 2009 scholarly volume on the cartoon controversy that was to have included reproductions of the controversial images, the university objected and, at the last minute, the Press decided to refrain from reproducing the images—evidence of the atmosphere of a creeping self-censorship in Islamic matters on both sides of the Atlantic.

At stake then was a conflict of principles—freedom of speech versus respect for religions. Yet European free speech has long claimed for itself the right to satirize and to criticize, especially, ecclesiastical authority. Caricatures of Islam are, on face value, equivalent to caricatures of Christianity, which make up a staple of European satire. To prohibit the one would inevitably imply prohibiting the other. Furthermore, the protests against the publication tended to conflate, erroneously, one Danish newspaper with the power of the Danish state. This can be taken as a symptom of what Ellian identified as an intra-Islamic predisposition to conflate religion and politics, which, he argues, is at odds with the Western tradition of a separation of spheres and a balance of powers.

Yet this cultural account of the dispute cannot evade the political issues at stake. Parts of the European public were recoiling from violence carried out in the name of Islam, from 9/11 to the assassination in Amsterdam. This identification of a new political violence with Islamist rhetoric—recall Bouyeri's imagery of death and destruction—was layered simultaneously on top of some more diffuse concerns with growing immigrant populations that were seemingly reluctant to inte-

grate. This problem grew all the more acute as some Europeans, especially in Denmark, began to move toward positive
evaluations of their own national identities and traditions,
which indeed implied a rejection of a multicultural immigration agenda. (This dynamic indicates a further dimension altogether: as some Europeans grew increasingly skeptical of
the process of integration into the European Union, they consequently moved toward a greater insistence on national integrity and particularity, and this in turn could mean a reduced
willingness to embrace immigration. From this point of view,
however, the acceleration of immigration ought to be regarded
as part of the agenda of the European Union to subvert and
eliminate the cohesion of national communities.)

It is worthwhile to give closer consideration to some of
the original twelve illustrations that seemed to cause so much
offense. At least five of the cartoons should be regarded as
primarily self-referential to the extent that they specifically
reflect on the process of drawing, on the artists, on the *Jyllands-Posten,* or on Danish politics. That group puts less emphasis on the image of Mohammed than on the processes or
frames of image-making itself. Three others address questions
of gender equality. Two (the man in the desert and the profile
with the crescent moon) seem innocuous enough, and neither
could be demonstrably proven to be a representation of Mohammed: not every bearded face is a prophet. Of course, the
Jyllands-Posten publication entitled the set "Mohammed's
face," but it would be difficult to defend that designation as
an accurate account of the images.

One image that has, however, been singled out for particular criticism depicts a man wearing a turban with a bomb in
it: whether the man is Mohammed, the symbolic association
of a turban (taken inaccurately to signal a Muslim) with vi-

olence is surely not illogical in the context of the events of the previous years. Islamist rhetoric—at least since 9/11, although (had more attention been paid) long before that as well—had established an increasingly familiar discourse, in which Islamism, claiming to represent Islam, derived a mission of violence from the Koran. It is not as if some of the cartoonists and parts of their public simply invented an imaginary association of Islamism and violence all on their own. If parts of the Western public succumbed to the erroneous association of Islam in general with violent Islamism in particular, then some of the responsibility for that "Islamophobic" conclusion has to be laid at the door of the Islamists themselves and their apologists. In fact the insistence by Islamists that they represent the violent core of Islam only reinforces the Islamophobic thesis that similarly equates Islam and violence.

The controversies in the Netherlands and Denmark have much in common. Of course, there was a vigorous debate in each country, and opinions were spread across a spectrum. When all is said and done, however, the Dutch public sphere failed to rally around the defense of Ayaan Hirsi Ali. True, the case was complex, and she had misrepresented herself on her initial asylum application. However, one is left with the impression that many in Holland were happy to catch her in this error, and they resented the fact that her advocacy for women's rights disturbed the lazy peace of a multiculturalist accommodation with abusive behavior in immigrant communities. The Dutch abandoning Hirsi Ali was appeasement politics in the cultural sphere. They were happy to see her leave their tranquil world. The resistance to Hirsi Ali—on the part of the Dutch, not the Islamists—epitomizes a European reluctance to defend freedom. Perhaps this reluctance was particularly strong in Holland, given its failure in Srebrenica. Perhaps, however, the same moral indolence defined both the refusal to act in Srebrenica and the abandonment of Hirsi Ali.

The Danish public reacted differently. Some Danes, of course, did complain that *Jyllands-Posten* had engaged in provocation and sensationalism. However, by and large, the government and the public stood by the principles of free speech and refused to compromise, displaying a muscular defense of freedom. This is another side of contemporary European culture, and it is therefore not surprising that Danish troops play a brave and important role—not encumbered by the exceptions claimed, for example, by the Germans—in the war in Afghanistan. The confrontation with Islamism involves domestic cultural conflicts as well as international obligations. The European encounter with Islamist terrorism takes place on distant battlefields but also in the streets of Amsterdam and Copenhagen. It is important to think through the different fronts. A reliable ally in wars abroad ought to demonstrate a reliable culture and an appreciation for freedom at home. Denmark is an exemplary case.

CHAPTER SIX

Bosnia

Genocide and Terror

On September 10, 2008, a civil court in The Hague dismissed a case against the Netherlands that had been brought by Hasan Nuhanovic, a survivor of the 1995 Srebrenica massacre who had been employed there as a translator by the Dutch battalion. Fleeing Serb forces, Bosnian Muslims sought refuge in the UN camp, and the Dutch allowed 5,000 to enter, but left many more, perhaps 20,000 outside. As Nuhanovic recounted in an interview, "They closed the gate. They sealed a hole in the fence. . . . If you were inside the base, you were safe because the Serbs did not do anything bad to the people inside the base. I heard about killings happening outside the base. I heard screams and shots. I was afraid, of course, for my family, my parents and my brother—if they stepped outside the base, they were going to be killed. So I tried to keep them inside the base." Yet eventually the Dutch forced the refugees out, turning them over to the Serb forces: "Some of the people, when they reached the gate, saw the Serb soldiers standing there next to the Dutch soldiers, pushing the men and the boys away from their sisters, wives, children—there was a separation taking place right there at the gate. People actually realized at that very moment that something is wrong, thinking, 'I'm not going to any safe place. The Serbs are going to take me.' The Dutch just stood there. Some of them turned around and walked back toward the factory [where the refugees were gathered inside the base] and forcibly expelled them."

Nuhanovic survived in the camp only because he held a UN identification card, but his parents and younger brother were murdered, sharing the fate of the other refugees. In the aftermath, he has tried to pursue the matter through the courts, claiming that the Dutch, acting as UN forces, had failed to protect the population in the UN "Srebrenica safe area." In particular, the UN failed the Bosnians Muslims who sought refuge in the compound of the Dutch battalion (or "Dutchbat") as Srebrenica was falling to the Serbs on July 11, 1995.

The court in The Hague denied Nuhanovic's claim with the stunning assertion that once the Dutch forces began to act for the UN and fully complied with UN orders, they were no longer compelled to fulfill any further international expectations to which the Netherlands might otherwise be obligated: "The court rejects the assertion that after the transfer of the relevant powers of control and command to the United Nations it still needs to be tested whether the State complied with its obligations under the human rights treaties, the Genocide Convention, and the Red Cross conventions (Geneva conventions)." In other words: once the UN assumed control of the Dutch forces, all those treaties lost applicability, even though the Netherlands was a signatory to the respective agreements. Transfer of authority to the United Nations, as the organization of international governance, evidently cancels nation-state responsibilities. The court goes on: "If in the execution of powers which the State no longer has, standards are violated, then the point of departure should be that these violations cannot be attributed to the State. The European Convention on Human Rights (ECHR) is not applicable according to the court because the United Nations are not a contracting party and the citizens of Srebrenica did not come under the jurisdiction of the Netherlands."

This argument has to be savored: the Dutch forces at Srebrenica did not have to fulfill obligations stipulated in the European Convention on Human Rights because they were acting for the United Nations, which is not a party to that convention. That the UN War Crimes Court had determined in 2004 that the Srebrenica massacre constituted genocide made no difference. Evidently, in the view of the court, entering into service of the UN has the legal consequence of voiding international accords, in particular, standards of human rights. Indeed, the judgment proceeds to argue that the Dutch might only be held responsible if they had contravened UN orders. Since the Dutch had, let us assume for a moment, respected superior orders, they are, in a remarkable post-Nuremberg twist, absolved of responsibility. They were just following orders. The case provides telling corroboration for political philosopher Hannah Arendt's deep-seated skepticism of human rights and international governance. It is extremely unlikely that any political power will come to the defense of stateless populations. The corollary to that statelessness of the victims is the abdication of state responsibility through a flight into the fictions of international governance. The broken promise of safety in Srebrenica is a melancholy allegory for the failures of European political will and the incapacities of the UN. If Muslims disbelieve the ideals of the West, it is perhaps because the West chooses not to live up to them.

The scope of the failure became apparent in the court's response to a parallel case brought by a group called "Mothers of Srebrenica," representing victims and widows. Would the court do justice to the victims? Apparently not. The same court which, to Nuhanovic, claimed that the UN and not the Netherlands was responsible, also declared that the UN enjoys absolute sovereign immunity, based on the 1946 Convention on the Privileges and Immunities of the UN, and therefore cannot be held responsible for actions undertaken "for the fulfillment of its purposes." Attorney for the plaintiffs, Axel Hagedorn, commented that it is unacceptable "that the UN is the only organization in the whole world that is uncontrolled and has absolute powers and therefore stands above the law," and expressed the intention to appeal to the European Court of Human Rights. As it stands, he argues that the judgment asserts that "the Genocide Convention is less important than the absolute immunity of the United Nations [which] means that the United Nations soldiers can do whatever they want and you can never charge them. So the victims, the relatives, the Mothers of Srberenica are without any rights."

The Srebrenica massacre, designated a genocide by the War Crimes Tribunal in The Hague and the International Court of Justice, continues to cast a long shadow. Haris Silaijdzic, a member of the Bosnian presidency, visited New York in 2008 and in an interview expressed apprehension about steps to admit Serbia into the EU as long as Serb war criminals remain at large, particularly Ratko Mladic, the general responsible for the Srebrenica killings. Against this background, the Dutch court's verdict appears all the more callous, an evasion of responsibility shrouded in the fluffy idealism of the United Nations. The complicity of Europe in genocide received judicial approval. "I have repeated thousands of times that I am not here to blame Dutchbat for their passivity," Nuhanovic hammered back. "I am accusing them of being active—in violation of the human rights of my family and other refugees. I noticed the judge read several times the sentence 'under the UN flag.' They referred to the flag under which these Dutchbat actions were conducted. However, these actions were conducted under the flag of the Netherlands as well." Both flags were flying, but for the court neither indicated responsibility. On the contrary, they cancelled each other. To Nuhanovic's case against the Netherlands, the court argued that the UN was responsible; to the "Mothers of Srebrenica," the court claimed that the UN operated beyond any responsibility and was therefore immune to criticism.

In the Wake of the War

From this point of view, a plausible lesson to be drawn from the war in the Balkans and its recapitulation in the court case is surely the unreliability of Europe as a site for its own most cherished cultural values: normative justice, human rights, humanistic modernity—the register of venerable ideals is not deemed sufficiently worthy for Europeans to act in its defense. One is left with a sense of fecklessness, on the one hand, and disappointment on the other. For if, as has been argued in previous chapters, the most effective response to the potential of Islamist terrorism in Europe would be to offer the Muslim immigrant populations the opportunity to integrate into mainstream cultures animated by a strong sense of the values of modernity, it is hardly reassuring to have watched Europe choose not to act in defense of its purported values, even in the case of genocide on its own territory. The same Europe which, domestically, is stymied by a cultural relativism that prevents it from articulating a forceful defense of its own heritage, has proven itself at best an unreliable partner in foreign policy as well. There are exceptions, to be sure, such as the disproportionate role that Danish soldiers have bravely played in Afghanistan. If, however, there is an apt symbol of what to expect from Europe in the defense of freedom against terror in the world today, it is not Danish courage in Helmand but Dutch enervation at Srebrenica.

In the wake of Serb terror against the indigenous Muslim population, the future of Bosnia is important as a possible marker for the paths of Islam in Europe. To be sure, Bosnian Islam is hardly typical: it is a long-standing cultural community at the intersection of Europe's Christianities, both Roman and Orthodox, and the legacy of Turkish Ottoman rule. The centuries of interfaith and interethnic negotiations in Bosnia provide a rich background, so thoroughly different from the experience in Western Europe of new immigrant populations from the Muslim world. Yet Bosnia is not on an island; it is not isolated from the rest of the world, and the collapse of Communism, the forces of globalization, and the radicalization of Islam have not passed it by.

What are the Bosnian options, what cultural options are available?—in the wake of Communism, in the wake of genocide, and in the wake of the failure of Europe and the UN to prevent the trauma of mass killing. The collapse of Yugoslavia, the war and genocide, and subsequent processes have contributed to redefinitions of Bosnian identity and culture, which also intersect with other international transformations involving the politicization of Islam and networks of terror. The Western European behavior during the war, the

extraordinary hesitation to act in the defense of the beleaguered Muslim population, and responses such as the court
decisions in The Hague hardly send an inviting message to
the Muslim world. On the contrary, they can credibly be understood to indicate a decisive rejection of Muslim Bosnia—
not a rejection of immigrants, nor a rejection of Turkey (as a
potential member of the EU), but of Europe's own. It is not
difficult to speculate that a plausible response to that rejection
could include shifts in Bosnian identity toward a redefined
Islam and possibly even toward an Islamism with a potential
for terrorist radicalization. That is certainly not the necessary
outcome of postwar Bosnian cultural developments, nor is it
even a likely outcome. Yet this potential casts Bosnia as a
foil to the immigrant populations discussed in the earlier
chapters, where "homegrown" terrorism could emerge in the
disaffected immigrant communities of Western Europe. In
Bosnia, the questions involve the aftershocks of the war and
the genocide: the character of political arrangements and local
cultural meaning in postwar Bosnia; analyses of international
terrorism and global security questions; and wider interroga-
tions of traditions and liberalism within the cultural contradictions of modernity, the frame to any significant discussion
of the tragic interplay of genocide or terrorism.

It is to that dialectic that a discussion of Bosnia in this
context necessarily points: genocide and terrorism, two extremes that stalk the utopias of modernity. Terrorists, we
know, resist modernization, even as they make use of modern
technologies, and the civilized world condemns genocide for
not living up to the principles of a humanistic modern world.
But these are two questions that seem to track modernity, step
by step: even as modernizers try to make the world a better
place, they unleash these twin forces of destruction. Of course,

the nexus of questions around the genocide of Bosnian Muslims in the mid-1990s is distinct from the post–9/11 concerns
with Islamist terrorism, but they do not exist in separate
worlds. The conceptual differentiation between them becomes
hard to maintain once one begins to take a closer analytic look
at terrorist networks.

Bosnia has come to figure, along with Chechnya, Palestine, and Kashmir, as an example of Muslim suffering, an
image of victimization that serves the purposes of jihadist recruitment. The killings in Srebrenica, which the Dutch failed
to prevent, provide the rationale to convince young men from
places like Molenbeek to travel to Pakistan for training. Bosnia was a particularly important crossroads in this story. Arab
veterans of the mujahadeen war against the Soviets in Afghanistan eventually made their way as fighters to Bosnia.
These so-called "Wahabi," as they were called in Bosnia, less
because of their theological sophistication than their funding
source, remained relatively independent from the Bosnian military structure, waging their own brutal war against the Serbs.
The mujahadeen also brought with them a much sharper and
more disciplined form of religious practice than characterized
the Bosnian Muslims. Given this connection, it is difficult to
maintain the distinction between the Bosnian genocide and
Islamist terrorism. The narratives are different, but they inter-
twine: all the more reason for caution about efforts to appropriate the material for competing political agendas. While
jihadists invoke Srebrenica to justify their violence as self-
defense for beleaguered Muslims, Serb nationalists have a
vested interested in associating Bosnian Muslims with radical
Islamists or foreign powers. Milorad Dodik, the prime minster
of the Serb Republic, regularly designates Sarajevo as "Tehran," suggesting both a growing Islamization in the erstwhile

multicultural city and, specifically, the influence of Iranian funding.

This is where the analysis becomes complex and treacherous. Without endorsing Dodik's mean-spirited denunciation, one can nonetheless concede the credibility of the reports of an increasingly Muslim Sarajevo. This cultural change has multiple causes, of course. It is due as much to the departure of members of other ethnicities, as to the international emigration of the secular urban population with a concomitant influx of more traditionalist rural Bosniaks. In addition, there may have also been a quite plausible and sincere turn to religion as a response to the trauma of war and genocide. Into this mix, all pointing toward an intensified Islamic identification, enter the genuinely international components: the influence of the "Wahabi" fighters—many of whom remained in Bosnia, despite the provision in the Dayton accords that they leave—and the generous funding from Iran and Saudi Arabia.

One especially salient impact of that funding is the transformation of the architectural landscape of mosques throughout Bosnia. During the war, numerous mosques were destroyed, a cultural dimension of ethnic cleansing. Since the war, many have been rebuilt or, rather, frequently enough replaced with new constructions of a significantly different style. Instead of the traditional, often small store-front–sized mosques of the Ottoman period, the new edifices, such as the King Fahd Mosque just outside of the center of Sarajevo, are enormous and starkly modern, arguably conveying a different sense of Islam, quite distant from the lax, modest, and comfortably provincial Islam that had earlier constituted the "Bosnian Way." The new mosques radiate a sense of imperious power coupled with an austere asceticism, devoid of any play-

ful ornamentation. They embody a sort of modernist international style at odds with local traditionalism. How this for-
eign-funded reshaping of the architecture of Bosnian Islam
impacts the lived experience of religious culture goes beyond
the scope of this inquiry. Suffice it to note, however, that
Islam in Bosnia is, literally, beginning to look different as it
simultaneously undergoes a significant integration into international and specifically non-European networks, much more
so than had ever been the case before the war. And this in-
ternationalization of Islam in Bosnia, coupled with a more
aggressive posture, could be an early warning sign of a new,
mobilized, post-traditional faith.

Islam, Islamism, Intolerance

These complex pressures on Bosnian Muslim identity need
to be considered within the range of paradigms that have
developed, especially since 9/11, to understand connections
between Islamism and political violence. At one end of the
spectrum, there are accounts rightly designated as Islamophobic, in the sense that they derive terrorist behavior directly,
indeed simplistically, from core Islamic texts. In this version,
exhortations to violence in the name of religion in the ancient
scriptures are sufficient causal explanations of contemporary
terrorist violence. The basic structure of the argument involves
locating passages that appear to authorize violence in the
name of Islam and then proceeding on the assumption that
the modern Muslim reader of the text necessarily carries out
the message, without interpretation or reflection. The clear
flaw in this sort of account, however, is that it assumes that
the reader acts automatically, never interpreting or nuancing
or rethinking ancient wordings in modern settings. Ultimately

this approach leaves no interpretive space between text and recipient and lends its imprimatur to the most literalist readings. The sad irony is that the Islamophobic critic in effect agrees with the most extreme fundamentalist on the meaning of the text.

At the other end of the range of accounts of Islamist violence, apologists insist on denying any substantive connection between religion and violence: Islamist terrorism, in this version, has nothing to do with Islam at all. This refusal to consider a religious genealogy to violence emerges, in some instances, out of a liberal discomfort with treating religion as anything other than a fully private matter. The presumption of an absolute wall between church and state is taken to prohibit any reference to religion with regard to a political event. Alternatively, the refusal to address the religious connection may simply reflect a tendentious agenda to excuse and to instrumentalize the acts of terror by shifting attention to political grievances. Pursuing political agendas, Western advocates prefer to minimize the importance of religion and focus public attention exclusively on political issues (for example, American foreign policy or the conflict in the Middle East). Yet such explanations for terrorism are deeply flawed insofar as they willfully disregard the speech of the terrorists themselves, who in fact do invoke sacred texts to vindicate their behavior. If the terrorists' verbal accounts do not necessarily provide an exhaustive explanation of their own behavior, it is hard to see why they should be treated as irrelevant. Osama bin Laden claims to act in the name of Islam; it would be surely odd to discount his own statements.

The truth must lie somewhere between those two poles. Some perpetrators of violence claim to act in the name of Islam. Determining whether they do so rightly or wrongly can be left to theologians. More germane, especially when we ponder how to respond to Islamist terror, is an inquiry into how particular cultural settings lead to different interpretations of the tradition and how different traditions solve political problems in varying ways.

This is where Bosnia becomes an interesting case: because it is a European site with a long-standing Muslim population (in contrast to the immigrant population clusters in West European cities), because its variant of Islam is understood by many as traditionally nondogmatic and tempered by close interaction with other faith traditions, but also because of the distinct legacy of the war experience after the breakup of Yugoslavia. How does that complex background, the loss of legitimacy of Europe as a cultural model and the suffering of the genocide, impact on the culture of Bosnian Islam and the potential for radicalization? Preliminary answers can be found in some recent cultural material: a festival, two films, and the writings of a distinctive public intellectual. As with any cultural analysis, there is no conclusive answer but only hints of future developments. Examining these different sorts of texts provides an opportunity to tease out some questions in contemporary Bosnian cultural developments: postwar, post-European, and postmodern.

On September 24, 2008, the long-planned Sarajevo Queer Festival opened with a photography exhibit at the Academy of Fine Arts. Intended as a celebration of a liberal and multicultural city, it was, however, greeted by a hostile and violent protest demonstration. According to Amnesty International "dozens of young men attacked participants, injuring eight people (including police officers)." According to other reports, festival attendees were not only attacked at the site but were also followed by cab across the city and assaulted elsewhere. The organizers were forced to cancel subsequent events, which had been planned to last for several more days. Was this the first sign of the intolerance of a resurgently Muslim Sarajevo?

It is important to recall the context—that attacks on gay parades had taken place in previous years in both Belgrade and Zagreb, so the issue of homophobia in the Balkans is hardly restricted to Bosnia. In addition, the hostile campaign waged during the lead-up to the festival spanned ethnicities. While prominent imams issued denunciations of the gay festival, so did representatives of other religions. As Bosnia specialist Peter Lippman reported, "Representatives from Bosnia's other ethnicities got in on the act, providing a rare instance of agreement across ethnic lines: The general secretary of Milorad Dodik's party, the SNSD, said of homosexuality that 'it is unnatural, sick, and deviant behavior.' Bosnian Croat politicians and clerics voiced similar opinions." Clearly the antipathy to homosexuality and the festival was not a matter of solely Muslim homophobia.

Nonetheless, a prominent feature in the public justifications for the opposition to the festival involved the scheduling of the festival during Ramadan. Should the planners have given greater consideration to religious sensibilities? Yet for the progressive community in Sarajevo, the very suggestion that freedom of expression should be contingent on religious sensibility was itself offensive. It would suggest a painful curtailment of hopes for an open society in Bosnia, evidence for which was provided amply by Bakir Izetbegovic, son of the former president and a political leader in his own right, who commented: "It's their [the gays'] business what they do, but they shouldn't popularize it, and display it as an innocent thing; that's a thing that spreads, if you let it. It should be kept behind four walls." For Izetbegovic, the resistance to the festival not only involves hostility to homosexuality but a broader sense of "traditional values." The movement against the festival was more than homophobia; it entailed a resistance to the cultural modernity that the festival would have represented and which was taken as an affront to Ramadan and Islam. In addition to this generalized ethno-religious structuring of the public discourse with regard to the festival, reports indicate that, on the level of activism—who really was in the streets demonstrating, which thugs did the bashing—"Wahabi" elements played a prominent role in the violence.

As noted, Sarajevo has hardly been the sole venue for homophobia in the Balkans. Yet while elsewhere anti-gay violence involved fringe hooligan elements, and while such criminal elements also reportedly participated in the Sarajevo violence, the opposition in Sarajevo reached well into the midranges of public discourse, and it operated with an emphatic invocation of religious identity and "traditional values." Tram stations were covered with posters with Koran quotations denouncing homosexuality. Ramadan became an excuse for anti-gay violence—hardly the case in Belgrade or Zagreb—that moreover was linked to a rejection of the West (the festival was funded with donations from Western embassies, including, ironically enough, the Dutch).

Homophobic attacks certainly do take place in Western Europe, and they reportedly involve immigrant youth. Yet the riot that ended the Sarajevo festival involved a public demonstration of homophobia on a different scale, a mob violence rather than individual attacks, wielding a considerable blow to the proponents of a liberal image of the city. A commentator in the local *Start Magazine* worried that "The cancellation of the Queer festival is a defeat for this city and for the dream of a multiethnic and multicultural Bosnia. . . . The world has been sent a picture of intolerance, extremism, and religious exclusiveness, and the whole story about Sarajevo's famous tolerance and multiculturalism has been reduced to a tragic-comic level." The truth of contemporary Sarajevo, however, is that it includes precisely this type of aspiration for liberal modernity alongside advocacy for traditional values and even proponents of religion-inspired violence. Which tendency will win out is a matter for predictions, but Sarajevo has become a test case for the future of a European Islam.

One might reasonably ask how much significance to attribute to this single event. Against the background of the Balkan tragedies, the cancellation of the Sarajevo Queer Festival was a small incident, no doubt, but measuring anything against genocide necessarily robs it of significance, so that is surely the wrong metric. As a symptomatic moment, the resistance to the festival indicates at the very least a flaw in the image of tolerant Sarajevo, and as the previous quotation indicates, it certainly represented a defeat, on the local level, to the hopes for modernization. Part of the interpretive complexity approaching postwar Bosnia involves the shifting frame from Muslim victimization during the war to victimization in the name of Islam, although again the difference in scale is overwhelming. For Izetbegovic the memory of the war ought to overwhelm and preclude the cultural liberalization implicit in the festival. "The violence is worse than any sexual depravity. But I think that . . . they [organizers of the Queer Festival] shouldn't do that in Sarajevo, you know, Sarajevo went through a lot of suffering, and that's a mainly Muslim population. This kind of thing makes them afraid."

Does the mandate to respect the victims indicate the imperative of maintaining an illiberal culture? Izetbegovic defines Sarajevo as a conservative Muslim city, a far cry from modernizing hopes as well as from memories of prewar urbanity. It seems to provide a distant echo of Ahmadinejad's notorious declaration regarding the absence of gays in Iran. Yet that comparison runs the risk of lending credence to the propagandistic denunciation of Sarajevo as "Tehran." At stake in the interpretation of the fate of the festival is a calibration of the encounter between liberal modernization and repressive religion in the capital of Bosnia. If the Queer Festival might be understood as an effort at a symbolic introduction of what might be designated as the culture of Amsterdam, that liberal icon, into Sarajevo, can one attribute the failure of the festival and the resistance to it as a consequence of the war, the role of the Dutch, and the failure of Europe in Bosnia's hour of need?

Genealogies of Terror: Two Films

Two films from postwar Bosnia allow for some further inquiry into the question of a continuity between the experience of the war and a cultural turn away from modernity and toward religion: Danis Tanovic's *No Man's Land*, which won the Academy Award for Best Foreign Film in 2001 and *Grbavica* by Jasmila Zbanic, awarded the 2006 Golden Bear at the Berlin Film Festival. Set in 1993, in the midst of the war, *No Man's Land* takes place largely in a trench, between the lines, where two soldiers, a Serb and a Bosniak, are forced to confront each other and, with considerable difficulty, find some few ways to cooperate. Yet *No Man's Land* provides no optimistic account of reconciliation; both adversaries end up shot. At the center of the plot, however, is a third soldier, a wounded Bosniak who has been placed on top of a pressure-release mine: if he moves, it will explode, and this mine is tellingly and explicitly identified as having been manufactured in Europe. Against this backdrop, the film displays the confused and unproductive responses of the various UNPROFOR forces: the French sergeant who disobeys orders by trying to help; the British commander who lies in order to save face; the German bomb expert who, unable to defuse the bomb, sits by the victim in embarrassed uselessness. In the end, all depart, soldiers and journalists alike, leaving the soldier on his back, on the mine, as the soundtrack cuts to a lullaby, and a sweet voice sings of a lost kingdom, an allegory of Europe's abandonment of Bosnia. The failure of the international community, portrayed with biting satire, leaves Bosnia to regress into an identity embodied by a folksong, as it rejects the Europe of technological modernity, political corruption, and media frenzy.

In contrast to *No Man's Land*'s dark humor, *Grbavica* offers a more conventional drama, the exploration of a mother-daughter relationship in postwar Sarajevo. Twelve-year-old Sara believes that her father had died as a Muslim martyr, a "*shaheed*," on the battlefield fighting the hated "Chetniks," the derogatory designation of the Serbs. Eager to participate in a school outing, she learns that the trip fee could be waived for orphans of martyrs, if appropriate documentation can be provided. Eventually her mother, Esma, is forced to admit the truth: Sara's father was no martyr. On the contrary, we learn that Esma had been raped in a prison camp, and the father, far from a hero, was nothing other than the hated enemy. Despite this inauspicious revelation, strangely enough, all ends well, mother and daughter reconcile, and Sara departs with her classmates singing a happy song about Sarajevo, "Land of My Dreams." Yet more important for our purposes, two sequences, both in a women's center for rape victims, shed light on the Islamic transformation of postwar Sarajevo. In the first, Esma participates in the gathering solely for financial reasons: women who attend the session receive a government welfare payment. Otherwise, the gathering has a solely perfunctory character. One woman laughs hysterically while others recount their stories, and there is a general atmosphere of alienation, boredom, and insincerity (although the character of the laughter testifies to the unresolved gravity of the underlying trauma). The second sequence, by way of contrast, conveys an aura of sacred devotion and spiritual consolation, through a prayer song with a compelling repetition of "Allah."

At stake then in *Grbavica* is the status of religious, specifically Islamic, markers: the terminology of martyrdom and the turn to prayer. Neither element seems informed by anything like an elaborate theology but both function instead as symbolic indicators of community membership. Yet both markers also respond specifically to the war. Religion is the answer to the suffering endured. Just as *No Man's Land* leaves the soldier regressing to a folksong at the moment of death, *Grbavica* stages Islam as a vehicle to interpret and surpass the grief of rape warfare. Religion provides comfort to the victims of suffering, hardly implausible, but this claim would provide greater credibility to Izetbegovic's challenge that wartime suffering and religious sensibility deserve respect.

There is a further ambiguity in the film's exploration of the value of martyrdom. For the schoolchildren, the "*shaheed*" has no particular theological content, and it appears to be untainted by any specifically Wahabi influence. Yet the orphans nonetheless maintain a significant investment in the term, which is associated with sundry emblems of violence:

for example, a revolver shows up even at a moment of tender teen romance. While the optimism at *Grbavica*'s conclusion is surely intended to convey a happy-ever-after mother-daughter bond, the martyrdom question is left troublingly unresolved. A potential for free-floating violence begins to circulate in the film's depiction of Sarajevo. In a cleverly tongue-in-cheek shot, a group of gangsters plot a murder, while the viewer sees one of the new modern mosques looming in the background. There is, the film suggests, some connection between Islam and violence. Does the theological emptiness of the martyr concept make it more easily accessible to manipulation by ideological agendas? Could an embittered Sara be recruited by charismatic mujahadeen who could become the heroic father figure she misses?

The various materials discussed display alternate but complementary relationships between modernity and religion, and between Western Europe and Bosnia. The outcome of the Nuhanovic case in the Netherlands underscores the gap between the norms of international justice at its most liberal—the absolute defense of the UN—and the lived experience of the victims of genocide. In the controversy surrounding the closing of the Queer Festival in Sarajevo, one finds a generalized homophobia as the terrain of resistance to a progressive modernization as well as an invention of Islam as a vehicle for a populist resistance to cultural change: it remains an open question whether the eruption of violence specifically around a sexual-identity topic derives from the prominence of sexualized violence in the war. While *No Man's Land* provides a satiric denunciation of the international world order in order to close with the hopelessness of a regressive utopia, *Grbavica* rediscovers religious contents as enabling a positive surmounting of suffering, but it leaves an energized and forward-look-

ing youth equipped with an ominously indeterminate terminology of martyrdom. Will the celebration of the *shaheed*
eventually return as terrorism?

Rusmir Mahmutcehajic provides some productive guidance through this field of questions. Born in Stolac in 1948,
he studied in Sarajevo, received a doctorate in Zagreb, and in
the 1980s, served as professor and dean of electrical engi-
neering at the University of Osijek in Croatia. A dissident in
the Communist era, he was elected vice president of Bosnia-
Herzegovina in 1991 and served as minister of energy, min-
ing, and industry, but withdrew from government offices by
1993 in protest against the plans, later ensconced in the Dayton accords, for an ethnic division of Bosnia. His copious
publications since then involve efforts to rescue the idea of
Bosnia as characterized specifically by a mixture of plural
traditions, constantly interacting with each other, and therefore
opposed to the various agendas for ethnic segregation, which,
however, he sees tightly linked to deleterious aspects of modernity. Bosnia provides an opportunity to study deep-seated
fissures and insufficiencies in the modern world with ramifications that extend far beyond the peculiarities of the Balkans.
On the contrary, in his work he reads Bosnia and its vicissi-
tudes as an allegory for the possibilities of modernity more
broadly.

For Mahmutcehajic, the extensive international attention
on Bosnia since the war has focused only on the devastation,
offering up merely a repetitive "ritual of shame." This perspective, however, necessarily occludes Bosnian cultural
particularity and its specific advantages, since it is "the only
European country that throughout its history has been entirely
based upon a unity of religious differences, the very differences that are central to the peace and stability of the world

of the coming millennium." If Bosnia is served up here as a metaphor of difference, it is certainly not meant in the sense of the standard multicultural advocates of progressive modernization. One has to place the emphasis on Mahmutcehajic's identification of specifically "religious" differences. His Bosnia is the venue of a complex religious life, with multiple strands, but in which Islam functions as the encompassing shelter for the other Abrahamic traditions: this is very much about theology, not cultural diversity. In other words, the claim is not that Bosnia provided a territory in which multiple traditions could coexist, but that Bosnia at its essence was nothing other than the dynamic intertwining of faiths, "the potential created when several sacred laws and ways are present together."

While the war takes the shape of attacks on Bosnian Muslims by powers identified as Orthodox or Catholic, these are, for Mahmutcehajic, in fact political nationalisms, not religious contents. It is not religion that causes war (the causality claim that provides the foundation for much of liberalism) but rather political nationalism that manipulates and disfigures religion. "While justification was sought and found in the West's distorted image of Islam, the political ideologies of these attacks were based on the totalitarian conviction that an abased standard of ignorance and fear should be universally applied." This ignorance is precisely the eradication of religion, and the neo-totalitarian attack on religion singles out the Bosnian Muslims not because of any particular doctrinal dispute but because of the characteristic capaciousness of their Islam. This modernizing flattening of identity is the real threat to Bosnia, especially when, tragically, a symmetrical development unfolds on the Muslim side as well: "Precisely the same outlook is now being touted—with the support and funding of external sources—among the Bosnian Muslims . . . to prove to them that their religious identity contradicts the concept that Bosnia should embody the unity of different sacred traditions." The logic of the war proceeded via the genocide of the Muslims, but its goal was the elimination of Bosnia itself, understood as the precious site of religious richness. This religious suppleness, moreover, represented a threat to the bad logic of modernity inimical both to religion and to suppleness. Its outcome would be a desiccated, one-dimensional identity.

Mahmutcehajic develops this account, in some ways a post-Communist retracing of the itinerary of Critical Theory, through a discussion of tradition that combines phenomenology and theology in a critique of liberalism. The emancipatory hope first inherent in the Enlightenment's pursuit of autonomy undermined the authority of tradition and, with it, the value of the guidance tradition can provide, without any significant enhancement in intellectuality. In a distant reprise of Moses Mendelssohn's answer to Immanuel Kant on enlightenment, he argues that the elimination of traditional values unleashes a potential for evil in the name of modernization, which takes its most characteristic form in nationalism. Hence a brutalization of Bosnian identity has taken place as well, as the Bosniaks themselves ended up participating in self-destructive ideologies of national ethnic purification.

For this, Mahmucehajic lays the blame on the Bosnian political elite which opted for strategies of ethnic partition, with the practical consequence that those social types willing to carry out the violence came out ahead: "Thus, the mafiosos and the criminals of the Bosniac nation, who found themselves able to win cheap favor and status by murdering other nationals, were closer to the Bosniak political elite than were those people, of all nations, who tried to defend Bosnia as a state of all its peoples." The project to eliminate Bosnia was nothing less than the effort to extinguish that model of diverse humanity and multiple paths to the divine. "Human salvation lies in differentiating between the nonreal and the real, and the choice of, and adherence to, the Real: the paths differ, but the end is the same. The desertion or denial of any one way is a denial of the end: it is a denial to humanity of the possibility of salvation."

By now the Bosnian challenge to Europe has taken on an unexpected significance. It goes far beyond policy disputes over post-Communist state-building or intercultural problems of multiethnicity or even the role of the United Nations. It is rather about a revalidation of religious tradition against secular modernity through Mahmutcehajic's account of Bosnian Islam. To be sure, his critique of modernity is not aggressively antiliberal, indeed he seeks a reconciliation of liberalism and faith, and he therefore stands at an infinite distance from the antimodernism of jihadist critics of the West. Yet he demonstrates forcefully that a profound crisis of European culture is underway, one indicator of which is the resurgence of religion, part of which is Islam, and a part of that is Islamist jihadism. To understand the jihadist critique and the potential for terrorism therefore requires grappling with the cultural contradictions of modernity itself.

In a final turn in his argument, Mahmutcehajic takes the battle of ideas to one of the iconic sites of modernity, the concluding passage of Max Weber's famous speech "Science as Vocation," and the dramatic contrast between "old churches" and "intellectual integrity." While Weber touted the value of rationality over the deficiencies of any irrational traditionalism, Mahmutcehajic deems neither option adequate to the tasks at hand. The historical moment calls instead for the instatement "of an order in which the truth might manifest itself as salvation for the human openness toward the signs in the outer horizons and the inner selves." Yet neither quantitative science nor the nationalistic deformations of "old churches" are sufficient. Indeed the "old churches" have distorted their own traditions by collapsing into nationalism. Both legacies—bad science and bad faith—have therefore contributed to the continuity of killings and the genocides of modernity. Simplistic worldviews both, their proponents are inevitably compelled to simplify the world and eliminate complexity.

Mahmutcehajic's critique of Weber leads to a rejection of the "arrogance of science" that distinctly echoes the Communist-era dissident discourse that attempted to subvert the "science of Marxism-Leninism" with appeals to the transcendence of phenomenological horizons, now shifted into a religious register. The reified worldview of modernity, its pursuit of an imminent "heaven on earth," can distort religion as much as it can impoverish science: the unholy alliance of modernity with an "old church" is a convincing working hypothesis for an explanation of Islamism as one more dead end. Only a different modernity, one open to transcendence, might provide an alternative.

After our examinations of the various Western European societies and their encounter with Islamist terrorism, Bosnia looks like a very different case indeed. Its history with Islam is much longer and indigenous, and its recent experience with war and genocide has no recent parallel in the West. Yet many of the familiar elements are there, albeit in a very different mix: social displacement, the tensions in modernity, the temptations of heroic violence in the name of redemption. Bosnia is a distinctly local case, but one that is thoroughly implicated in international networks—the role played by Western Europe and the United States in the war, the emigration of so much of the population, the influence of Saudi and Iranian funding, and the trails of the mujahadeen fighters. The answers from Bosnia are also reminiscent of the discussions in the West: if only modernization would take root, if only resentment would give way to a productive integration into a free society, terrorism would fail. Yet where the Bosnian case points in a new direction is the way it raises the question of religion, not only as a negative, a backwardness, a flaw to be corrected, but potentially as an important component of a productive and stable society sustaining human dignity and sustained by sacred traditions.

This perspective sharpens the discussion of the encounter with Islamist terrorism in an important way. We have taken pains to underscore the need to distinguish between Islam and Islamism: a failure to do so will undermine the war of ideas against terrorism because it will push the whole Muslim world into the Islamist camp. Yet that strategic calculation is not the crux of the matter. Rather, one singularly narrow interpretation cannot lay claim to a full tradition. That reductionism, distorting the richness of faith into the dogma of a closed-minded ideology, would amount to precisely the one-dimensionality against which Mahmucehajic warns. But if Islamism is not Islam, there is still one more step to take. That distinction is ultimately just the particular case of a more general claim: religion cannot be reduced to religious violence, and therefore a rejection of notionally religious violence—the war on Islamist terrorism, for example—is not a war on religion at all. There have to be ways to rediscover the civilizational value of the sacred and retrieve it from the hands of fanatic murderers. The jihadists' critique of modernity involves the claim that the West has no values and, ultimately, no God. Bosnia asks whether the West can prove them wrong.

Afterword

The shock of 9/11 stunned the world and a brief moment followed full of extensive solidarity with the United States. The sight of the collapsing towers truly did elicit genuine sympathy from many quarters, but that instant passed quickly. The standard narrative, however, according to which the Bush administration squandered that allegiance is not tenable. From the morning after the attacks, long before U.S. policy even took shape, there were voices calling for the United States to refrain from responding at all or even offering the quickly stereotypical and deeply offensive interpretation that the attacks were a legitimate response to American foreign policy. The age of anti-Americanism had begun. It was not the Bush administration's deeds but rather the attacks themselves that had unleashed the torrent of abuse directed at the United States. Once Al Qaeda had wounded America, others, especially in Europe, felt authorized to give expression to their own, previously latent animosity. The very fact that the United States had been hit and hit badly produced the rage of anti-Americanism; the cause did not lie in the policies that the

United States would pursue in response but in the wound itself.

Once the United States did begin to act, influential politicians like Jacques Chirac in France and Gerhard Schröder in Germany used the opportunity to profile themselves against Washington, part of their own opportunistic electoral calculations. Given their prestigious positions, their choices provided further cover to the wave of hostility to the United States that swept through Europe in those years.

That wave has been subsiding for the past few years. Perhaps this was due to a changed tone in Washington during the second Bush administration, as diplomacy became more successful. Perhaps Europeans grew skeptical of the credibility of their own anti-American leaders' integrity: in retrospect it seems that Schröder's politics were driven by his own well-laid plans to find a career, after the chancellorship, working for Vladimir Putin's Gazprom, and Chirac's involvement in corruption charges returned to the headlines once he left the presidential office—neither a paragon of civic virtue by any means. Yet a much more important component of the changing European perspective has been the gradual realization in Europe that the world is indeed a threatening place, and that Europe is especially exposed to some geopolitical dangers. The American post–Cold War withdrawal from positions in Western Europe that it had held since 1945 left the continent more vulnerable to a renewed Russian assertiveness. Yet falling into Moscow's orbit is hardly an attractive fate. Even more ominously, Iran's dogged pursuit of nuclear arms has embarrassed the Europeans' efforts at diplomacy and, ultimately, has added another very real threat to Europe's capitals, but not to the American homeland, well beyond the reach of Iranian missiles.

Above all, however, Europe has had to face the reality of Islamist terror in its streets. In September 2001, Europeans might have felt comfortable in the delusion that Al Qaeda was only a scourge to the United States and some presumably indulged in the unkind speculation that the United States had only itself to blame. That cozy innocence is gone. Europeans have faced their own terror: the bombings in Madrid and London, the suitcase bomb in Germany and the Sauerland trial, the murder of van Gogh, the riots in France, the anti-Danish violence and repeated threats against politicians and intellectuals who dared to speak out. Europe discovered its homegrown problem, and it became Europe's turn to find a response to terrorism.

That response has been complex, varying from country to country and across the political spectrum. The renowned German author Martin Walser has called for a withdrawal of German forces from Afghanistan, while, in contrast, the British prime minister, Gordon Brown, has been far ahead of President Obama in calling for enhanced forces to carry out a surge strategy. The Italian government cooperated closely with the United States in the 2003 apprehension of a key terrorist recruiter, Osama Moustafa Hassan Nasr, but an Italian court has now convicted 23 American agents for helping transport him to Egypt, even though the rendition had been approved by the Italian government itself. German interior ministers, on the right and the left, have pursued tough policing measures, going well beyond the Patriot Act, but in Britain similar measures, promoted by the Labor government, have encountered opposition on both the left and the right. In France and Germany, new discussions about promoting national identity have developed, as alternatives to the multicultural past, in the interest of integrating the immigrant population, but in England a quintessentially multicultural proposal, the assimilation of sharia law into the British legal system, has been promoted by none other than the Archbishop of Canterbury.

So the European response has been by no means monolithic. Europe is after all broad, with diverse cultures and traditions, and the various countries have had different experiences with terrorism. The individual chapters in this book have attempted to tease out some of the national specificities in the reactions to terrorism. Yet an overall picture has emerged as well and it has ramifications for the future. Four points in particular with policy implications need underscoring:

- Europe has grown increasingly concerned about Islamist terrorism. Its resistance to the war on terror has begun to wane in light of its own experience with terrorism and its fears of renewed attacks. This changed perspective has reduced the anti-Americanism that seized Europe in the first years after 9/11.

- Europe is concerned with signs of disaffection in its immigrant populations where homegrown terrorists might be recruited. Its answer should be to pursue policies that accelerate integration and that reduce the sort of cultural segregation promoted by obsolete multiculturalism.

- Some European countries have developed highly successful counterterrorism institutions that may have useful lessons for the United States. Transatlantic cooperation in counterterrorism has to be maintained as a high priority. Reports of growing recruitment from Europe and the

United States to training camps in Afghanistan, Pakistan, and Somalia should be taken very seriously.

- A public case has to be made for the coherence of policies on three different levels—the war in Afghanistan, domestic counterterrorism, and immigrant integration. All three represent responses to Islamist terrorism, and they should be defended as a package. Otherwise objections to each individually—on the basis of pacifist opposition to the war, absolutist insistence on the priority of civil liberties, and cultural-relativist multiculturalism—will undermine the comprehensive strategy.

Yet beyond policy, we should not lose sight of the fundamental terms of the battle and the values at stake. Since 1989 and the opening of the Berlin Wall, all of Europe is democratic. The continent is home to a set of prosperous, stable, and free societies. Of course, they are not without their problems, and some of these problems have been touched upon in this book. There can be no doubt, however, that the freedom at home in Europe is a remarkable good. That good is under attack by an Islamist extremism that couches its hatred for modernity in an idiosyncratic interpretation of religion. The danger of that jihadist agenda should not be underestimated. We know how much suffering it can cause and how it is willing to use violence against innocent civilians. The war against Islamism in Europe is a war for free societies everywhere. It is not a war against Islam, nor a war against religion, but a war against a specific ideological extremism hostile to the free societies of modernity. Some Europeans are waging that war with dedication and seriousness. It is important that they win that war, despite the resistance they may face from other Europeans, distracted by other ideological commitments. The United States should support Europeans in their confrontation with violent Islamism, learn both from their errors and their accomplishments, and recognize their battle as our own.

Suggestions for Further Reading

For readers interested in pursuing the issues raised in greater depth, the following list offers some suggestions. Some of the titles concern terrorism, some focus on European culture. The list includes political essays as well as works of fiction. It is far from an exhaustive bibliography and only presents volumes available in English. All the material listed here sheds light on the problem of contemporary Europe's response to jihadist terrorism.

Ali, Monica. *Brick Lane: A Novel*. New York: Scribner, 2003.

Amis, Martin. *The Second Plane: Terror and Boredom*. New York: Vintage, 2008.

Bawer, Bruce. *While Europe Slept: How Fundamentalist Islam Is Destroying the West from Within*. New York: Anchor, 2007.

Bawer, Bruce. *Surrender: Appeasing Islam, Sacrificing Freedom*. New York: Doubleday, 2009.

Berlinski, Claire. *Menace in Europe: Why the Continent's Crisis Is America's, Too*. New York: Three Rivers Press, 2007.

Berman, Paul. *Terror and Liberalism*. New York: Norton, 2004.

Brisard, Jean-Charles. *Zarqawi: The New Face of Al-Qaeda*. New York: Other Press, 2005.

Buruma, Ian. *Murder in Amsterdam: Liberal Europe, Islam, and the Limits of Tolerance*. New York: Penguin, 2007.

Caldwell, Christopher. *Reflections on the Revolution in Europe: Immigration, Islam, and the West*. New York: Doubleday, 2009.

Fallaci, Orianna. *The Force of Reason*. New York: Rizzoli, 2006.

Hirsi Ali, Ayaan. *Infidel*. New York: Free Press, 2007.

Houellebecq, Michel. *Platform*. New York: Vintage, 2002.

Ibrahim, Raymond. *The Al Qaeda Reader*. New York: Broadway, 2007.

Küntzel, Matthias. *Jihad and Jew-Hatred: Islamism, Nazism, and the Roots of 9/11*. New York: Telos Press, 2007.

Laqueur, Walter. *No End To War: Terrorism in the Twenty-First Century*. New York: Continuum, 2004.

Laqueur, Walter. *The Last Days of Europe: Epitaph for an Old Continent*. New York: St. Martin's Griffin, 2009.

Henri-Lévy, Bernard. *Left in Dark Times: A Stand Against the New Barbarism*. New York: Random House, 2008.

Nuhanovic, Hasan. *Under the UN Flag: The International Community and the Srebrenica Genocide*. Sarajevo: DES, 2007.

Mahmutcehajic, Rusmir. *Learning from Bosnia: Approaching Tradition*. New York: Fordham University Press, 2005.

McEwan, Ian. *Saturday*. New York: Anchor, 2005.

Philips, Melanie. *Londonistan*. New York: Encounter, 2007.

Pipes, Daniel. *The Rushdie Affair: The Novel, the Aytatollah, and the West*. New York: Birch Lane, 1990.

Ratzinger, Joseph, and Jürgen Habermas, *The Dialectics of Secularization: On Reason and Religion*. Fort Collins, CO: Ignatius Press, 2007.

Ratzinger, Joseph, and Marcello Pera, *Without Roots: The West, Relativism, Christianity, Islam*. New York: Basic Books, 2007.

Rushdie, Salman. *The Satanic Verses: A Novel*. New York: Random House, 1988.

Suljagic, Emir. *Postcards from the Grave*. London: Saqi Books, 2005.

Thornton, Bruce S. *Decline and Fall: Europe's Slow Motion Suicide*. New York: Encounter, 2007.

Tibi, Bassam. *The Challenge of Fundamentalism: Political Islam and the New World Disorder*. Berkeley: University of California Press, 2002.

Tibi, Bassam. *Islam's Predicament with Modernity: Politics, Religious Reform, and Cultural Change*. New York: Routledge, 2009.

Updike, John. *Terrorist: A Novel*. New York: Knopf, 2006.

Vidino, Lorenzo. *Al Qaeda in Europe: The New Battleground of International Jihad*. New York: Prometheus, 2005.

Ye'or, Bat. *Eurabia: The Euro-Arab Axis*. Madison, N.J.: Farleigh-Dickinson University Press, 2005.

About the Author

Russell A. Berman, the Walter A. Haas Professor in the Humanities at Stanford University, is a senior fellow at the Hoover Institution.

Berman specializes in the study of German literary history and cultural politics. He is a member of both the Department of German Studies and the Department of Comparative Literature at Stanford. From 1992 through 2000 he served as director of the Stanford Overseas Studies Program. He is currently chair of the Department of Comparative Literature.

He is the author of numerous articles and books including *Enlightenment or Empire: Colonial Discourse in German Culture* (1998) and *The Rise of the Modern German Novel: Crisis and Charisma* (1986), both of which won the Outstanding Book Award of the German Studies Association (in 2000 and 1987, respectively). Hoover Press published his book *Anti-Americanism in Europe: A Cultural Problem* (2004). His other books include *Cultural Studies of Modern Germany: Representation and Nationhood* (1993), *Modern Culture and Critical Theory: Art, Politics and the Legacy of the Frankfurt School* (1989), and *Between Fontane and Tucholsky: Literary*

Criticism and the Public Sphere in Wilhelmine Germany (1983). He has published numerous articles in *Hoover Digest*.

Berman has received many honors and awards including a Mellon Faculty Fellowship at Harvard University (1982–83), an Alexander von Humboldt Fellowship (1988–89), and the Bundesverdienstkreuz of the Federal Republic of Germany (1997).

Berman received his B.A. in 1972 from Harvard and his doctorate from Washington University in 1979.

Herbert and Jane Dwight
Working Group on
Islamism and the
International Order

HOOVER
INSTITUTION
STANFORD
UNIVERSITY

The Herbert and Jane Dwight Working Group on Islamism and the International Order seeks to engage in the task of reversing Islamic radicalism through reforming and strengthening the legitimate role of the state across the entire Muslim world. Efforts will draw on the intellectual resources of an array of scholars and practitioners from within the United States and abroad, to foster the pursuit of modernity, human flourishing, and the rule of law and reason in Islamic lands—developments that are critical to the very order of the international system.

The Working Group is chaired by Hoover fellows Fouad Ajami and Charles Hill with an active participation of Director John Raisian. Current core membership includes Russell A. Berman, Abbas Milani, and Shelby Steele, with contributions from Zeyno Baran, Reul Marc Gerecht, Ziad Haider, R. John Hughes, Nibras Kazimi, Habib Malik, and Joshua Teitelbaum.

Index